Photography

Race, Rights and Representation

Photography

Race, Rights and Representation

Mark Sealy

Lawrence Wishart
London 2022

Lawrence and Wishart Limited
Central Books Building
Freshwater Road
Chadwell Heath
RM8 1RX

Typesetting: e-type
Cover design: River Design
Cover artwork/photo credit: Samuel Fosso, *African Spirits* series (*Angela Davis*), 2008
Courtesy JM Patras / Paris
Printing: Imprint Digital

First published 2022
© Mark Sealy 2022

The author would like to thank Autograph ABP, London and
University of the Arts London

AUT⊙GRAPH

ual:

British Library Cataloguing in Publication Data.
A catalogue record for this book is available from the British Library

ISBN 978-1-913546-33-5
E Format 978-1-913546-34-2

Contents

Future-Facing People

Experiments with Time

Photography: Promises to Make a Revolution

This book is dedicated to
Shona Illingworth, Alina and Sonny Sealy.

Introduction

The texts in this collection were generated over thirty years working as a curator of photography and director of Autograph UK, or Autograph, The Association of Black Photographers as it was known in 1988 when it was founded. They are assembled here as free-floating forms of enquiry, time bandits from past conversations concerning race, rights and representation. When they were first written, they were not aligned to a fixed photo-orthodoxy, they simply existed. In these hostile times, they serve as reminders of how vigilant we have to be in defending social justice and political change. Collected together, they are cultural offerings that attempt to give voice to historically marginalised perspectives within photography.

Photography is omnipresent, sensorial, multidirectional; a layered and fluid creative process, it permeates and resonates across our planet in myriad forms, whether commercial, artistic or domestic. Many photographers, scholars and artists have served, in different ways, as key sources of inspiration for me. The work Roland Barthes produced in *Camera Lucida: Reflections on Photography* has been a constant influence across my writing, as has Suely Rolnik's essay 'The Body's Contagious Memory: Lygia Clark's Return to the Museum' more recently. Rolnik's notion that an 'imagosphere' surrounds the entire planet is an increasingly real and frightening proposition.[1] The writings of Stuart Hall, Kobena Mercer, Frantz Fanon, Sven Lindquist and Ariella Aïsha Azoulay all play in the background of my thought, as do the photographic works of Rotimi Fani-Kayode. The curatorial and historical research work produced by Deborah Willis has, over many years, also been a constant companion.

The brilliant Nina Simone reminded us, 'Jazz is not just music, it's a way of life, it's a way of being, a way of thinking'.[2] Recognising a sensory or disruptive, jazz-like aspect to the experience of photography can free us from the confines of Eurocentric epistemes, which function mainly to contain, fence off, frame, map, collect and claim ownership of all the meanings an image might produce, both aesthetically and logically. Jazz as a thought process unsettles dominant Western structures. Through its improvisational qualities, jazz creates space for a continuous and more globally inclusive form of expression. Applying this to photography, we can work towards a more spontaneous and receptive way of thinking that opens up space for sensing and feeling the work that a photograph generates across different individual, temporal and cultural experiences.

Within this space of unanchored and evolving meanings, the process of reading an image can be freed from fixity and an obsession with making truth universal, thereby allowing repressed knowledge(s) to emerge. In this more improvised world, knowledge, feeling and intuition merge with the rhythms of praxis, and the sacred and profound can be revered as living entities. Not fully knowable, they are evolving cultures or ever-present forces that open up new understandings and spark processes that can undo colonising confines.

Colonising institutions, their machines and methods of operation, create restrictive, all-consuming and dehumanising borders. These borders 'are not only geographic; they are racial and sexual, epistemic and ontological, religious and aesthetic, linguistic and national. Borders are the interior routes of modernity/coloniality and the consequences of international law and global linear thinking.'[3] These confined spaces of colonial control create the perfect conditions in which the politics of cultural erasure can thrive.

Western museums behave like Gods. They appropriate and make new truths from stolen objects and images. Their curators – the high priests – cast aside, devalue and devour the culture of Others for entertainment and profit. In this environment, the objects and images that get buried in the trivia of the museum remain culturally dislocated and unstable.[4] Museums denigrate that which they do not understand, but photographs refuse to be contained. In our entangled, increasingly digital, cultural world, photographs are infinitely reproduceable ghosts that haunt those who have tried to hold them captive or erase their presence through epistemic control.

Collectively, the bodies of works discussed here function as missing chapters, black chronicles or lost scores, sometimes at rest but often trapped in between official histories of photography. Once the images and the photographers who made them are allowed visibility, they eerily call back into existence difficult times that may have been buried or locked out of discourse, or abandoned to a space of non-caring. Photographers from different cultural backgrounds have, across the history of the medium, been curatorially absented, dodged and burnt out of photography's 'decisive' historical moments.[5]

Maganbhai Patel was also known by his community as 'Masterji', meaning 'honourable master'. The photographs that he made in Coventry after his migration from India are a testament to the photographic studio as a place of new identity formation and liberation. For nearly fifty years, he photographed in a frequency few outside of Coventry were tuned into. With the support of his daughter, Tarla, and local scholars Jason Scott Tilley and Benjamin Kyneswood, Masterji achieved his first solo exhibition in 2016 at the age of ninety-four. Through his photographs, South Asian migration to Coventry is recorded in a new, visual form that will persist in history.

The photographic works that I have been drawn to often address turbulent events that have either not been seen or have been systematically ignored. Photographs in this context, as Mariana Enríquez explains, are ghosts. They can 'scare you because they are full of rage. My [photographic] ghosts are angry, and they are angry because they have been ignored and because what has happened to them has been ignored not just by one person but by society; the system, and the only way to break that silence [is] by screaming.'[6]

The works of Maud Sulter, for example, scream at the past because their core purpose is to arrest the long arc of injustices that have eradicated black women from history. The series *Les Bijoux* that Sulter produced in 2002 is an exquisite set of nine, large-format Polaroids dedicated to the life and work of Jeanne Duval, the long-term companion of the celebrated French poet, Charles Baudelaire. In discussing the work Sulter stated, 'My ongoing visual fascination with Jeanne Duval began in 1988 with a visceral response to a Nadar photograph captioned Unknown Woman. There she stared at me willing me to give her a name, an identity, a voice. So for over a decade I have been image-making with her in mind.'[7]

Sulter's art is grounded in a form of photographic excavation work that evidences forms of Eurocentric disavowal concerning connections with Africa. Through this process, Sulter makes black women central in Europe's histories.

In this collection, I have engaged with artistic and photographic histories by visiting the familiar and seeking out the unfamiliar in the body politic of cultural production, where words become images and images become words, where bodies become signs and signs become bodies. Images, like the written and spoken word, transmit cultural knowledge, fuel memory and root a people's sense of themselves in a place. In thirty years working at Autograph, and through never-ending, liminal approaches to curating photography, I have sought to make interventions that permit formerly colonised peoples a rooting in time and place.

Many of texts presented here have been produced through decades of work to resist essentialising cultural positions and against the homogenising cultural fallout of the late 1980s, which saw state funding and modes of cultural production becoming disproportionately influenced by commercial forces. This was typified in the YBA (Young British Artist) phenomenon that became the default narrative across the arts in Britain. 'Different'[8] voices, those cast as being on the margins of British culture, especially black photographers, were effectively cut off from spaces in which to display their works. In Autograph, this meant that publishing and commissioning critical dialogues around black photographic works, especially those that addressed the difficult areas of race, rights and representation, became and still remains a vitally important site of engagement.

Time has shown us that photographs can signpost the escape routes from essentialising Western visual regimes. Different eyes prioritise different points of reference and in a radical curatorial pluriverse, a photograph's meanings would be encouraged to transmutate and shift over time. Latoya Ruby Frazier's photographs from her project *The Notion of Family* (2001-2014) visually forge into existence the effect of America's industrial decline and corporate greed on African-American families. As a body of images, they evoke a cross-generational sense of societal entrapment, especially for the black working class of Baddrock, Pennsylvania, Frazier's hometown. Ruby Frazier's project is produced through her family and with her community. It shifts the boundaries concerning classical black and white documentary work because at the heart of this project lies an autobiographical narrative that spans three generations of women's struggles against poverty, bringing sharply into focus the impact of race, class and gender on the body of African Americans.

Years earlier and on the other side of the Atlantic, Rotimi Fani-Kayode was producing an incredible, Other-worldly example of photographic hybridity, cultural alchemy and escape from his one-bedroom flat in Brixton. In his home-cum-studio on Railton Road, he unlocked the door to a new cosmological space. During his short career, he galvanised the energy of 1980s London, fusing notions of freedom and desire with different cultural and political elements that, when brought together through the experimental lens of his camera, changed the criteria for the representation of the black male body in photography. In this moment, something in the history of photography imploded; old traditions began to sink in on themselves like a black hole, while a new, African, transgressive, spiritual light simultaneously appeared in northern skies, first as a faint star but then as a burning sun that would come to be recognised globally. The hybrid, Yoruba, photographic cosmos produced by Fani-Kayode will forever be felt within photography. His work, like so many of the photographers discussed here, was generated within a time and space that John Coltrane called 'A Love Supreme', and was produced out of a deep and enduring passion.

When repressed knowledge is allowed a voice and then embraced, it helps us understand that nothing in the past is over and that time and history, when considered through photography, can and will be reworked. Photographs remind us that our histories and memories, whether traumatic or pleasurable, stay deep within the wells of our souls, where they wait for different triggers to release them. Photographs, then, are hot molecule agitators at work in the cool, dark corners of our minds, enabling what was locked away to resurface, goosebump-like, in our consciousness.

When we are caught off guard by the work a photograph does on our interior selves, the experience can be overwhelming. This was made evident to me in 1998 when I curated an exhibition at the Pitzhanger Manor and Art Gallery in west London to commemorate the fiftieth anniversary of the HMT Empire Windrush arriving at

Tilbury Docks. The photographs displayed of West Indian migrants arriving in Britain, along with a range of photographs showing World War Two West Indian service men and women, brought many of the visitors to tears. They were overwhelmed that their experience of migration and war service was being acknowledged through these exquisite historical photographs.

In his memoir *Familiar Stranger: A Life Between Two Islands*, the cultural theorist and long-standing chair of Autograph, Stuart Hall, reflected on the experience of seeing the exhibition: 'I was overcome by the emotional weight of images that surrounded me and by the memories of the varied fortunes of my migrant generation. We'd all undertaken the journey to our many illusions. Embarrassingly I found myself in tears'.[9] This account, more than any other, transformed my understanding of the importance of the documentary moment and the need to narrate our own stories.

Sunil Gupta is also an emotional time traveller. His search for love and equality has been rendered through a liberatory form of self-reflection and honesty. Photography has taken him around the world and beyond, stripping himself bare before his own lens, journeying, in his words, 'from here to eternity'. Gupta is caught in the matrix of time, space, family and desire. Being motivated by a sense of justice means that his photographic moral compass points with magnetic force towards challenging local and global social inequalities. His photographic episodes function as forms of visual baptism. They are immersive, transformational bodies of work that both inspire and act as agents for change.

Photographs, especially those designated as unimportant, those buried under the weight of time, those awaiting release from the fossil-like chambers and violent cultural spaces that house them, make real that which has passed. When photographs knead on colonial meanings and disturb our sense of humanity, reminding us of the pains people have endured and the gains they have made, they can help us to acknowledge that we must hold all the world's memories as precious.

The photographs that I am most intrigued by are the ones that help us to understand our dark pasts and to create the conditions where restorative, representational acts of care can be felt as well as seen. In this type of cultural care work, the many Others of the world, especially those subjected to and silenced by myriad forms of Western violence, may be seen and heard in our present, allowed to rest, but more importantly, to have a voice in times to come. This curatorial praxis operates as a form of resistance work that, word by word and image by image, aims to dismantle the brutal and universalising modernist mindset. It contributes to and builds on the forms of 'transdisciplinary education and knowledge production' needed to heal from the violence of Western visual regimes.[10]

Mark Sealy
2022

NOTES

1 Suely Rolnik, 'The Body's Contagious Memory: Lygia Clark's Return to the Museum', https://transversal.at/transversal/0507/rolnik/en, January 2007.

2 United Nations, 'Tenth Anniversary Celebration of International Jazz Day', www.un.org/en/observances/jazz-day, accessed 7 December 2021.

3 Walter D. Mignolo and Catherine E. Walsh, *On Decoloniality: Concepts, Analytics, Praxis*, Duke University Press: Durham, 2018, p112.

4 Ariella Azoulay, *Potential History: Unlearning Imperalism*, Verso: London and New York, 2019, p116.

5 Henri Cartier-Bresson, *The Decisive Moment*, Simon & Schuster: New York, 1952.

6 *Ghosts*, featuring Mariana Enríquez, in 'Hauntings', BBC Radio 4 Short Cuts, www.bbc.co.uk/programmes/m000mt18, 22 September 2020.

7 Maud Sulter, *Jeanne Duval: A Melodrama*, National Galleries of Scotland, 2003, p11.

8 Stuart Hall (ed), *Different: A Historical Context*, Phaidon: London and New York, 2001.

9 Stuart Hall and Mark Sealy (eds), *Familiar Stranger: A Life Between Two Islands*, Duke University Press: Durham, 2017, p174.

10 Clémentine Deliss, *The Metabolic Museum*, Hatje Cantz Verlag: Berlin, 2020, p63.

Photography,
Representation
and Jazz

1

On Being in Limbo

Mark Sealy in conversation with Elisa Medde

In the weeks prior to our conversation, Mark Sealy and I had been sharing emails discussing the idea of 'limbo' in photography and beyond. The state of being in temporary lockdown, with no background noise other than our households, seemed like the perfect condition to reassess, ponder and evaluate – as if a big noise cancellation function had been switched on.

This issue's core questions, 'What can photography do?' and 'What do we want to do with photography?', quickly became the foundation for a larger, more complex conversation: how do we address the limbo as a political reality? What kind of role and function lies within the experience of images and objects? What role and importance do images have for those trapped in the limbo, for example, for migrants carrying photographs as amulets sewn into clothes while crossing the sea?

The limbo has many connections with the Other as a state of being and as an enforced political state. Mark suggested that we need to 'unlearn any universal ideas concerning the knowledge an image may contain' in order to surrender to a visceral, almost osmotic type of knowledge that is informed by the experience of the image and, ultimately, by how much the image resonates with us. Then, tragically, George Floyd was killed by a police officer in Minneapolis, and the limbo all of a sudden got its audio functions back.

Elisa Medde: What's on your mind these days?

Mark Sealy: Since we spoke things got crazier, didn't they? I think this place of limbo is an important metaphor. At the moment we are nowhere, I would argue, because there is no leadership. It doesn't feel like we are going in any particular direction, it feels like a cycle of economies and tragedies. I'm trying to imagine what ways of being we could be. What could the future look like, apart from more technology? What is the future for human relationships that are tactile, that are loving, that are caring, that are educational and inclusive, diverse and accepting of all the nuances of the human subject? I'm interested in what photography can do to help us fundamentally understand new ways of being.

EM: What I find interesting now is this global momentum that we are witnessing.

I think partly it's because so many with the privilege of being able to isolate, not being essential workers, became obsessed in the pandemic with their own personal bubble. Many of us felt trapped, with reality suspended. And then, all of a sudden, a video lasting 8.46 seconds led us to reassess reality – it turned the audio on. People realised, perhaps naively, that life never stopped, and things started to be exposed under an unforgiving light.

MS: Absolutely. It's a long road to change, but I think the pandemic and the murder of George Floyd did bring things into focus quite sharply in many ways. Some people in our societies have been locked down for a very long time, not just by the pandemic. That created a perfect atmosphere for people to go out and demonstrate for theirs and other people's rights, against state violence, state controls, and the lack of state care for black people. I still shudder with disbelief at how many people die at the hands of the police globally. It draws attention to the way that many regimes use violence against those whose lives they render worthless. It's great that the Black Lives Matter Movement has become the driver for greater human rights globally, especially for those who have been historically oppressed.

EM: In Europe, countries are witnessing internal movements pushing to come to terms with their historical and systemic blind spots. It's happening in the Netherlands, in the UK, in Belgium, and each of them has different trigger points. In Italy, it all started because the general public was obviously outraged by the murder of George Floyd, or better, by the images of it, but then first, second and third-generation migrant communities started saying: 'You're outraged now, but no one flinches anymore when a boat filled with fifty or sixty migrants sinks at sea and images of dead five-year-olds stranded on the beach circulate widely.'

Then we have the video of George Floyd's murder, where the police officer's performance for the camera was straight out of the trophy-hunting tradition, a very specific composition and body language reserved for hunted animals, arrested outlaws, escaped slaves and tortured prisoners. The history of photography is filled with such images, and now videos. How can we connect this idea of the limbo as a political reality to the idea of the Other? What kind of role are the images playing here? Do they trigger, do they overload, how much and what kind of information are they conveying?

MS: Good question. I think the problem with photography is that its application is so eventful, it's so about the event, either a performative event, made in the studio, or captured events, what some people might call 'the decisive moment'. What would happen if we finally realised that when we're looking at photographs, they don't really help us see or understand what is happening in front of us, that photography might simplify everything? We have to remember to look outside the frame.

Photography's power for witnessing and presenting violence, and for being a tool that gathers critical evidence, is well documented. Now more than ever, the application of photography has to be forensic. It's more a case of 'How do we see?' and 'What do we see?' and 'What do we bring to the fore?' If people didn't have mobile phones then the George Floyd murder would have just been another unseen, violent statistic where a black man lost his life. We wouldn't have felt that moment of massive injustice. I think the reason the footage of George Floyd's murder is so vital is that it makes us feel something. It arches us back to centuries of violence against black people.

I think that unlearning the work images do when we look at them and responding and acting on how we feel is really central to what photography has to do now. Like powerful music, photography must take us somewhere beyond the act of seeing. I'm not arguing that we've seen too much, but I'm arguing that much of photography does not move or touch us anymore, and that's the point. Maybe we've lost the capacity to be moved, unless we consider the work the photograph does across culture and time. We need to pause, reflect and act differently on how images are read. I think, in this sense, photography can still be a liberating device.

You could argue that the recording of George Floyd's killing, the capture of that horrific violence, shows us how brutal people can be to those they hate, how violent and oppressive state agents can be. We are reminded of this in *Without Sanctuary* (1999); for many of us who are trying to read images alternatively, it's about the faces of the people in the crowd at a lynching. Part of the horror of the photographs is, how can you look at images of black people being so debased? The other part is, how can those crowds of people in the photographs be so happy? What is it, culturally, that makes it possible for them to hate so much?

EM: Isn't it the same conversation that started and then very soon stopped about the smile of the soldier on the Abu Ghraib images?

MS: Yes. The question is, where does that come from? What cultural generators are at work for that smile to happen? If we're going to tackle racism, that's the inquiry. Not just the act, it's what has been generated in our culture that propagates that level of hatred. I think debasing images still do that work. For example, if we don't know the names of migrants, if we don't understand the circumstances of their departure, if they're never on TV saying who they are, where they come from, or what they long for. Even if they were asked simple questions in a short news brief it would change the dynamic, by helping us understand the conditions of these people's lives.

When I see exhibitions with migrants as, if you like, the palette for artists to work with, I find that very challenging. Do we understand fully the complexities of their lives? Will we ever provide the platforms for that to happen? And what is the space in which the artist operates when addressing these themes? Artists like Fazal Sheikh have tried to do that, with his early project *A Camel for the Son* (1992-2000), but he is very much in the minority in terms of a methodology. It seems to me that, even after all this time, the preferred approach for rendering the migrant or the refugee subject is to objectify.

I criticise these methodologies because I don't think they move the conversation any further. They use the migrant body or the refugee body to make (often well-intentioned) interventions that are much more about the artists than the subjects in focus. It builds on narratives of making outsiders and this connects with the idea of being and constructing a non-person, the idea of being inside or outside of the state, a minus-class citizen (having to be marked, for example, by wearing a yellow star). Agamben talks about this, so does Foucault, in terms of understanding how rights work within the state and on the human subject, the idea of who is imprisoned, who is surveilled, who is inside, who is outside. Judith Butler also addresses this, as does Christina Sharpe and Claudia Rankine.

We're still in what Walter Mignolo calls the 'colonial matrix of power'.[1] Until that colonial matrix of power is broken and we start thinking differently, delinking and thinking apart from these traditional ways, we will remain trapped having the argument about the aestheticisation of violence. The challenge, really, for contemporary artists using photography is, how do we break with the old and build something new that really talks about the state that we're in?

EM: I feel that the problem is not about the quantity of images, or being desensitised by what you're seeing, but about how you're seeing it. This connects with the idea of contemporary images needing to be 'hyper images', living organisms. The future of the image is to be a living organism that works only if you are able to experience it, not just with your eyes but with your senses at large and with your soul. In the text for the catalogue of *African Cosmologies* (2020), the exhibition you curated for FotoFest in Houston that had to close right after the official opening due to the pandemic, you make a very powerful connection to jazz. These days, I feel thrown into an Albert Ayler album, as if it were 'Spiritual Unity' all over the place. Everything is so loud and so intense, but then you have these moments of clarity, sustained by very solid and clear foundations, in which everything makes sense.

MS: I think that's a really important point. You could argue that the horror of the killing of George Floyd was like a dart of reality that hit the emotional bull's-eye. We've been told we've all got to stay together to fight this virus, that we need a global response to it. Then these horrendous violent moments occur, and it really did ground people again into the reality of what black people deal with on a daily basis in relation to just living. It's horrendous in many ways. I think you're right about the idea of the background noise being wiped away. Sometimes things happen that we can understand instantly, and I think we may be in one of those moments. I think that's when you get a generational shift.

I like the idea that jazz is this kind of disobedient episteme; it goes off in tangents, you're allowed to just flow with it. It's not strict, but at the same time it has an underpinning structure that can hold things together. I'm looking for visual conversations that are able to go off on tangents, but at the same time have a kind of underpinning body politic within them that says something concrete about where we are. If you look at Rosana Paulino's work, there is something about the emotive, the historical, the contemporary within her work. The idea of stitching, embroidery and the intersectional conversations that happen through her work enable you to feel as though it's more than just a great photograph, it's more than just a great video. It comes back to a connection.

EM: When you say that it will be important and necessary to unlearn any universal knowledge an image might contain, and if we link this idea of unlearning to the extremely powerful, liberating sense of a sensorial experience of photography, would you argue that we need to shift our focus from the intellectual to the emotional? Or do we need to reshape our intellect as well? Our system, our ideologies of understanding?

MS: It seems to me that the knowledge systems generated by Western society are in crisis. Capitalism, wealth and violence go hand in hand. Whether it's the Spanish in South America or the Europeans in Africa, it has always been about extraction, hasn't it?

EM: It's the giant triplet: racism, materialism, militarism.

MS: Exactly, and people have become increasingly disposable in the aggressive turn to globalisation. Instead of people's lives getting better, they seem to be getting worse. Being poor in a really wealthy country seems to be a different kind of poverty. It's not like having to walk a mile to get some water. You are simply debased and left to become part of the disposable or waste byproducts that democracies like Britain or America find acceptable. You're left in the wasteland because there are always other people to come forward and do the job. There is a weird form of modern slavery going on, Kevin Bales talks about it in his book *Disposable People*,[2] and I think people are becoming more aware of it.

I think that knowledge systems as they've been generated in the West are becoming redundant and there are other systems that people like Walter Mignolo have been asking us to consider for a while. There is Indigenous knowledge, there are other ways of being, there are different forms of spirituality, different ways of sharing, different ways of making, different ways of telling stories. Of course, the more the planet dies, the more those knowledge systems come under threat, the less we learn and the more exposed we are to totalitarian regimes.

This idea of decolonising is about a plurality of epistemologies that we need to have in our armoury that we can all share, rather than the universal, as in the university, as in the Western academic trope telling us the way that it should be. I think we need to open up our minds to different knowledge systems. They can and will be spiritual. There can be counter-narratives to the way that Indigenous cultures around the world have been framed, and there must be a different form of empowering through these knowledge systems. It's valuing all those other knowledges that are part of us.

EM: Human culture.

MS: That's right, human cultures. Human culture can't just be a car, a nine-to-five job, a nice apartment, shopping on a high street and wearing designer clothes. They've sold us all of that for years and it doesn't work. Surely human culture is about how memory works, how relationships work, how we care for elders, what we do with our children, how family works, and how the local works within a global context.

EM: If we relate these thoughts to photography, then we can argue the space to act and interact in is quite broad.

MS: Definitely. If you look at the time of photography, it's interesting. It arrives at the height of imperial Europe, just before the division of Africa in Berlin. It arrives when Europe is trying to reign supreme, and when we see that, we understand that photography's history is a very dark place. Those that had the camera, what I will call the 'colonial camera', haven't helped us to understand the Other, or bridge these important human differences. It hasn't brought us closer together. So if we're going to break the limbo of where we are, this sense of being caught in unanimated space, then something new has to happen. A new direction and a new or recognized set of responsibilities has to emerge.

I'm still very thankful for Ariella Azoulay's *The Civil Contract of Photography*,[3] she and many others have been calling for this kind of responsibility for a long time. We do need to think about responsibility when we have these tools in our hands. What are we communicating? What for? When we look at the history of photography, the photographs as objects tell us much more about the photographer than the subject in the frame because the subject in the frame, in terms of our understanding of them, is mostly absent.

EM: We need to talk about a way of working, a praxis, a commitment for institutions, museums, magazines, curators, editors. It must relate with how you are telling stories, how you're presenting them to the public and how you are bridging the gap between the people organising these showcases of images and their reception by the public.

MS: Sadly, *African Cosmologies: Photography, Time and the Other* (2020) in Houston is under lockdown at the moment, but on the opening night, there were two distinctive moments. One when the exhibition first opened for a restricted invited audience, and a second wave around 8:30 p.m. when the general public were invited. Watching young, African Americans come in and literally dance in front of Samuel Fosso's photographs was an amazing moment. It was one of those few moments in curatorial work where you can really feel that what they are seeing is both self-affirming and politically poignant to them.

I would argue that in that exhibition, there is a lot of heavy, political work. But there is also an incredible amount of pleasure and complexity. Rotimi Fani-Kayode's work is there, Ernest Cole's work is there, which is all about pushing back on apartheid, framing the 'House of Bondage' he escaped from, talking about freedom, African spirits. There's a huge, complex, multi-layered image by Zanele Muholi, performing and linking to the struggle for workers' rights in South Africa; Depera's photographs where young Congolese in the 1950s are dressing as cowboys, having a great time, feeling as though they own the night. The complexity of the human subject is there for people to enjoy, and you could feel the pulse of that in the room. You could feel the difference it was making. You could feel the sense of pleasure in the atmosphere that people created in response to the work.

You could argue that people like Samuel Fosso, through his project *African Spirits* (2008), are talking to different types of audiences. This is not some African kitsch performance; it is about people being allowed to understand who Lumumba was and who Angela Davis is, and to celebrate them through Fosso's work. You realise that there is a visual deficit because we are bombarded with violence, so it's not surprising when people like Dawoud Bey or Carrie Mae Weems make work that has all of this poetry written into it, or Christina Sharpe and Claudia Rankine write about wanting to just be free to *be*. It is liberating in the same way John Coltrane and the move towards spirituality through jazz is liberating. People are looking for that as a form of escape from the violence that they live in. And I think only if you live that form of state violence can you feel what it means to long for solace.

EM: It is that sensorial experience we were talking about, which acts as a sort of exorcism? Is it a ritual that becomes liberating?

MS: Correct. I think that when disenfranchised communities go to museums, they often can't find a purchase. They can't see themselves in the space. I think this is the chance for museums now going forward. They have to change what's being collected, they have to change what's being valued, they have to diversify who's writing about the work, they have to offer new epistemes, new chapters, a new way of being, a new chronicle, new stories, to allow these narratives to flow from the other brilliant voices that are out there. It's more about dovetailing and joining these narratives together.

Our lives on this small planet are entangled, whether we like it or not. That was the point I was trying to make with *African Cosmologies* – contemporary African photography is everywhere! It's in the mix. What we need to do is change the way in which we embrace difference. Each time you go to look at a photograph, it means different things. But it means different things because we've moved on in time and place. If we go back to something, it's not exactly the same. We're seeing it differently because we've experienced a little more of the world, for example. So we might understand it differently, or it might become even more confused.

Part of the problem is that people want to imagine there is some kind of a recipe for understanding ideas. I think it only works if we allow for the possibility of new ingredients and for mistakes to occur. Due to pedagogic dictates, we are obsessed with making sense of images rationally rather than thinking, how does that move me? Yes, it is fantastic to be able to talk about and write about images, but it can't be fixed. It has to be felt and it has to be fluid. That's where we begin to build up a pluriversal rather than a universal way of understanding. 'What's the work the image is doing in culture?' is one of my mantras. A historical image from the civil rights movement is doing different work now to two weeks ago because it can remind us of the struggles that African Americans have been through, so it helps us trace how long the path to justice has been.

EM: Once you assess and grasp what photography can do, the inevitable next step is to decide what you want to do with it, what direction you want to go in.

MS: I think there is going to be a new, far more inclusive narrative around what photography does in culture. I think the challenge for us is around curatorial care. If you and I are running magazines or institutions, how do we care about things, including the things we don't understand? If we don't understand things, it doesn't mean we have to shut them out. We can be generous. We can bring in people who do understand those spaces, and help us all understand by opening up the pages, opening up the walls of our institutions.

There are artists now coming from the global South and there are sensitive curatorial spaces in Europe that are realising that, if they are to be relevant, they have to have a conversation with those artists. Eric Gyamfi is doing good work, we know that people like Carrie Mae Weems are still doing very important work. Going back to Rosana Paulino's work, think of the materiality within the work that is trying to literally join us together through radical women's quilt-making, bringing family stories together through patchwork quilts.

The problem with our universities is that they forget the patchwork nature of history. It becomes a homogenous, big square, and at the moment, it's a big, colonising square. What we're seeing is people wanting to change that, to enter into that frame, dilute it and realign it to make it something else, a space they can see at least part of themselves in. When you begin to see yourself in that space, when you begin to have a voice, have agency, have recognition, new meanings become possible.

This interview originally appeared in Foam Magazine *on 1 October 2020.*

NOTES

1 Walter E. Mignolo, Catherine E. Walsh, *On Decoloniality: Concepts, Analytics, Praxis,* Duke University Press: Durham, 2018.
2 Kevin Bales, *Disposable People: New Slavery in the Global Economy,* University of California Press, 2012.
3 Ariella Azoulay, *The Civil Contract of Photography,* Rela Mazali and Ruvik Danieli (trans), Princeton University Press, 2008.

2

Moments Outside the Frame

I have been talking to Sunil Gupta for over thirty years, if not more. Every time we speak it is a different kind of dialogue, a more enlightened one, as I increasingly come to understand him and his work. As we moved closer to the final stages of this exhibition,[1] our discussions became more a process of collecting recollections. The ephemera of his life facilitated this process and helped us comprehend what he looks for as an artist.

Being able to spend time with Gupta as we developed this project was a real learning curve, mainly because of his infectious sense of ease concerning turbulent pasts and how they intersect with pleasure. The past, for most of us, is an uneasy place to visit. It is the door that we are most reluctant to push open because we are never sure what might lie behind it. Curatorially, I think what is really interesting concerning the career of an artist like Gupta is the point where things began, the catalytic moments of making, the drivers that push people on in their lives to make them choose a life in and with politics. I see Gupta saying 'yes' to being a photographer as a radical act, 'yes' to being an artist and 'yes' to being a person who recognises that he needs to love to survive. Looking across his work, it is evident that the powerful undercurrent that ties all of it together is relationships.

The more I understand Gupta's praxis, the more I understand that his work, body and being are a creative marriage of the personal and the political, a commitment that hurts the heart and dizzies the head. Gupta's photography incorporates the big 'P' politics of social change, but it is also a life lived in politics that fuels his journey as both a leader and a follower through family, location and geography, through different kinds of communities, and across race, place and gender. At the soul of Gupta's practice, what connects his work to so many different constituencies is the idea of family, be it imagined or real.

Gupta's mother, Penny, was of Tibetan origin. Born, perhaps, to migrant workers in a tea plantation in Darjeeling, she was left behind in India, adopted by British missionaries and then moved out to boarding school. The missionaries gave her a solid education and by the time she had met Sunil's father, Shri Ram, Penny had a job, a bicycle and a home of her own. Penny was an independent, young, working woman, which was unusual for India in the 1940s. This independence was imparted to her son. Penny's life was not traditional in the Indian context, but rather marked a place of subtle rebellion. Sunil recalls that his Indian family did not have an extended network around them telling them what to do or how to behave. His early years were therefore quite liberal, free from tradition. The family then upped and emigrated to Canada.

Moving to Canada in 1969 allowed Gupta, then in his late teens, to discover his sexuality and forge an identity. Being part of the gay liberation movement meant that there was a critique of family structures – or at least the biological, heteronormative family – which was an uneasy and difficult situation for his migrant family to grapple with: 'They didn't quite understand why I wanted to move out and have a whole other life separate from them'.[2] But for Gupta, there was never a sense of complete separation because at the core of his family was a space of generosity and acceptance that he now recognises as being unusual.

The family had a deep understanding of what it meant to be an outsider. Both parents had been socially rebellious in their own way. His father had married outside his caste, which caused distress within the extended family. Gupta's grandparents refused to meet his mother for many years. Penny's Christian faith was a factor that worked against her being accepted. Penny's radical act was to marry a man who had been married before. In later years, Penny thought Sunil being gay was a way of God punishing them. Oddly, the family expanded slowly as Penny and Shri Ram enjoyed ongoing relationships with Gupta's ex-boyfriends, while current partners would be lectured for leading their son astray. I met Penny many times at private views and moments of celebration at Sunil's home. Her presence was always self-assured;

she welcomed conversation, especially with strangers, and had a powerful, quiet wit.

For Gupta, photography started in Canada through his connection with the gay liberation group at college. The group produced a paper for which they needed pictures and Gupta volunteered to be the photographer. He was interested in photography and it gave him a reason to take pictures and to organise his thoughts, to be present and, critically, to have an audience. Once a month he would have photographs credited and reproduced in the college's home-made *Gayzette*. This was a part-time occupation because he was supposed to be studying business.

That all changed when he arrived in New York in 1976, where he encountered a whole new world of photography possibilities; this is where Gupta's continuous photography started. In his classes, people talked about how everything needed to be photographed now. Gupta and his fellow students were encouraged to hit the streets and take tons of pictures. New York, it seemed, was open visually, waiting to be framed. In New York, as can be seen in his Christopher Street sequence, Gupta began to find a visual queer identity through a lens that became sharply focused on the exciting scenes unfolding on the streets as the queer world emerged into the daylight.

The Christopher Street photographs are important because they ooze with a desire and affirmation of a people on the move. Within each grabbed moment, you can almost feel the revolutionary disco of it all:

> I had never encountered anything like that before: so many galleries and so much photography happening. And it really aroused my interest in the sense that I'd been self-taught. But in New York I could actually meet luminaries from the photography world. I could take classes with Philippe Halsman who worked for *LIFE*, and with Lisette Model who taught Diane Arbus, and they persuaded me to take up photography. So I dropped out of business school and did more and more photography.[3]

On the emotional front, Gupta was following his heart: a relationship that had started in Montreal led him to experience queer New

York and then London in 1977. After being in London for a while, the Home Office caught up with Gupta and suggested he should leave the UK as he had overstayed his official visa. To enable him to remain in the country, he embraced photography further and enrolled on a three-year photography course at Farnham University for the Creative Arts in Surrey. Once he had completed the course, the Home Office made contact again, only to be informed by Gupta that he had enrolled on a two-year photography MA course at the Royal College of Art (RCA), London. Photography saved both Gupta and, more importantly, his relationship.

Britain in the late 1970s and 1980s was a class-based minefield primed by conservative racism and sexism. Homophobia was rife and London, for Gupta, after the euphoria of New York, was a difficult place to be. The gay scene was still primarily underground. Bars closed early and people were hostile to a young South Asian gay man. The police actively harassed the gay community through strategies of entrapment:

> People were trying to pick me up in a gay bar and the chat-up line would be a complaint about those Asians, why do they eat so much curry ... If only they didn't eat that food, that kind of thing. But it was meant in a positive light. They were trying to seduce me with that ... And so I still went out to take pictures, to look for something. I wasn't sure what until I found this kind of thing. This is a chance documentary picture in Battersea Park. I took it because it was about a black male posing proudly with his body on display, but it was also about the gaze of the two white guys. And so I guess photo theory had affected me in the sense of becoming conscious of who is looking at what and who is taking the picture for whom.[4]

London changed Gupta's photographic point of view. The city was divided across many fault lines and intersected by numerous different cultural fronts. The south bank of the Thames was home to the Greater London Council (GLC), which in the early 1980s was under the leadership of Ken Livingstone. London was a Labour Party stronghold that opposed, especially on the cultural front, the Conservative government led by Margaret Thatcher. Gupta made a crucial shift across the river to align himself with the left-wing progressive and inclusive policies of the GLC. He turned his back on the Cork Street art market agenda, for which the RCA had been grooming its students.

The pull towards the GLC was facilitated through Gupta's participation while at the RCA in a cross-disciplinary Asian, African and Caribbean student exhibition. The GLC arts officers were very keen and excited to meet these young graduating students who could talk the talk, who knew a bit about the system and who were interested in what they did. To understand the political making of Sunil Gupta, we also have to understand the radical politics of the GLC in the 1980s and especially the funding initiatives it undertook as it was facing the possibility of closure. Gupta

learned from them what that kind of politics means, how culture works, how funding works, how rainbow cultures of different, apparently diverse, but quite intersecting identities of elderly people, LGBT people, black people, Asian people can all come together under one umbrella. And then at the same time, we were having this shift from being called ethnic minorities to what was being called black. It was part of that postcolonial moment.[5]

The 1980s were also a transformative time for the family. Gupta did not return to India until the mid 1980s; he had been busy being an out gay man in London and that was simply not possible in India. But the death of his father in 1986 changed his relationship with India once more. The last time Gupta had seen his father alive, his father had made it clear to him that he felt Gupta had abandoned his responsibility in terms of looking after his parents. Gupta flew to Canada in time for the funeral and then took his father's ashes back to his uncle in India, where he, as the son, performed the ceremonial rites. Ironically, at the same time The Photographers' Gallery in London commissioned Gupta to produce a new series of photographs titled *Exiles* that focused on gay visibility in India.

By the mid 1980s, through the many different initiatives funded by the GLC, black artists from across London were beginning to meet each other for the first time. However, in 1986, the year that the GLC produced a number of cultural events under the heading 'The Black Experience', which included the important photographic exhibition *Reflections of the Black Experience* in Brixton, Thatcher's government abolished the Council, leaving a huge void in the multicultural landscape of London. Some of the gaps in the arts landscape, especially around photography and film, were filled by Arts Council England, leading to various reports and some funding opportunities.

Increasingly, Gupta became active across the independent (mainly publicly funded, not-for-profit) photographic scene in the UK, which consisted of a range of different facilities and spaces such as Camerawork in the East End of London; The Photographers' Gallery in Soho, London; Photo Co-op in Brixton, London; Impressions Gallery in York; Open Eye Gallery in Liverpool; and Side Gallery in Newcastle upon Tyne, all of which were dedicated to the display of photographic work and were sites where critical photographic work was being produced. This was complemented by publishing initiatives for photography such as the Birmingham-based *Ten.8* magazine and the London-based *Creative Camera*, both of which Gupta had developed relationships with.

It was within this turbulent climate of social and cultural change that Gupta and other activists such as David A. Bailey, George Shire, Merle Van den Bosch, Monika Baker, Armet Francis, Lance Watson, Michael Khesumaba Jess, Maxine Walker, Roshini Kempadoo, Prodeepta Das, Mumtaz Karimjee and Joy Gregory, among many others, battled to open up the space for organisations like Autograph: The Association of Black Photographers to exist. The political context of the independent photography scene also made this possible. It created the forums within which these important debates could exist and be articulated, as did the crucial support from Barry Lane, the Arts Council's officer for photography, and the brilliant work being done across the field of cultural studies, especially by Stuart Hall, who throughout the 1980s constantly demanded that the pathway for black creative lives be opened up.

Having encountered the steely black cultural politics of London, Gupta has returned to India again and again with a commitment not just to record and collect the experiences of Indian gay life but also to play an active part in campaigns to bring the right to consensual love onto the statute books. On 6 September 2018, a panel of

Supreme Court judges invalidated part of section 377 of the Indian penal code, thus making homosexuality legal in India.

2020

NOTES

1 *From Here to Eternity: Sunil Gupta. A Retrospective* (October 2020 – May 2021), The Photographers' Gallery, London, UK.
2 From a conversation conducted with Sunil Gupta on 28 July 2020. The conversation was hosted by Studio Voltaire, London.
3 *Ibid.*
4 *Ibid.*
5 *Ibid.*

3

On Joy Gregory,
Autoportrait (1989-90)

Joy Gregory's series *Autoportrait* (1989-90) was produced as part of the very first exhibition commissioned by Autograph and was shown at Camerawork in the East End of London in 1990.

This self-framing work was produced as a direct response to the lack of visibility of black women across popular culture and in particular the fashion industry. The success of this now celebrated 'body' of photographs represents a defining moment in British photography, a moment that can only be described as a politically charged and culturally defiant act. It was an act that placed gender, class and race centre stage in the contested field of representational politics.

2008

4

The Decolonial Logic

Stuart Hall's critical writing and political vision continue to be sources of influence and inspiration to generations of practitioners concerned with issues relating to cultural difference, displacement and power, as well as questions of race, history and memory. He played a seminal role in the conceptual and theoretical development of the work of many visual artists. Glen Ligon, Carrie Mae Weems and Isaac Julian are just a few familiar names in contemporary art that come to mind when we think of Stuart Hall's influence on the visual.

The idea of building a moving image project that is based on decentering the logocentric nature of Western thought through the prism of Hall's academic work on race and identity was initially discussed by Stuart Hall, Catherine Hall, Derek Bishton and me in a quiet café in Camden Town, London in 1998. The aim of the project was to explore the nature of the visual as a political trigger across an individual's memory landscape, both real and imagined, and to produce a multifaceted, immersive project that would allow people to see and feel what it means to live a life in politics.

This project was manifested in a commission for John Akomfrah to produce what would become *The Unfinished Conversation* (2012), a multi-screen work for Autograph that would incorporate a matrix of sound, still and moving images. Conversation with Hall would drive the production process, and Hall's personal archives would form the project's backbone. For Hall, this work would represent a visual space where a large degree of personal and cultural unpacking would take place. It would facilitate a stripping down of the elements of memory and time as well as the notions of family and a sense of place, ultimately resulting in an unveiling of the self. The project would take the audience on a journey beyond a single memory moment and join dots across the complexities of living in what I refer to as 'racial time'. As a concept, its core aim would be to address how the visual does its work on the subject and how political subjects could and should be read in different temporal moments. Indeed, the work would mark the diasporic personal prism that facilitated the thought of Stuart Hall.

The curatorial concept of building a wider exhibition project based on Hall's concept of encoding/decoding would lay emphasis on conflict within the visual, or at the least its asymmetrical relationship with the individual as a receptor who drifts across different cultural currents and personal spaces. The project's objective was to consider the physical and mental configurations of the cultural and political dynamics at play that operate simultaneously on and within the self.

This method of thinking involves a degree of image recall and interrogative history work, a process that appeals to many different artistic practices. It calls for non-prescriptive, non-linear readings of the past and demands that the kaleidoscopic condition of personal and cultural memory is forged into new and different formations. Here, political memory functions and agitates within personal and political space, positioning both the audience and the subject not as individuals fixed in any given moment, but as subjects continuously engaged across different spaces and times. Subsequently, audiences enter into constant states of personal and political flux, sliding seamlessly into and out of different identities, visual scenes and historical places of identity formation.

Given the fact that historical re-memory work, archive interventions and political restaging all form part of the natural palette of processes that artists draw from, it made sense to build on the work that Autograph commissioned. The curatorial objective of the resulting exhibition at The Power Plant, *The Unfinished Conversation: Encoding/Decoding* (2015), was to widen the visual conversations that Akomfrah's work on Hall opened up by including distinct historical and political voices that different artists had been in dialogue with. The exhibition's intention was to bring Othered political figures into the conversation through a process of invitation and deconstruction, with audiences becoming carriers of the potential meanings that each work in the conversation independently transmitted. Therefore, through the body of the audience, or transmitters, the film work of Terry Adkins in reanimating two great black American voices, those of Martin Luther King Junior and Jimi Hendrix, enters into dialogue with Sven Augustijnen's work on Patrice Lumumba; and in turn with Steve McQueen's work on Paul Robeson; Shelagh Keeley's project on the haunted colonial architecture of the Congo; and Zineb Sedira's fragile and weakened memories located in Mohamed Kouaci's intimate photographic archives, which represent the visual memory bank of the Algerian revolution. Effectively, the combined work produced by these artists becomes a meeting point across time for those who shared a desire to decolonise the world.

Collectively, *The Unfinished Conversation: Encoding/Decoding* aims to achieve a unique experience that utilises screen-based images, keywords, sounds and photography to create a visual and historical mosaic experience, working in the schisms across the field of identity politics, reproductive media and political memory constructs. The curation of this visual experience blurs boundaries between institutional and personal memory, revealing how one manages a journey through and into the question of the political self. It simultaneously offers a topology of politics that presents the opportunity to explore how discourse and moving image communicate politics as an agitated presence. Ultimately, *The Unfinished Conversation: Encoding/Decoding* as an exhibition is a process of acknowledging and reinforcing Hall's idea that 'reality exists outside language, but … is constantly mediated by and through language: and [that] what we can know and say has to be produced in and through discourse.'[1]

2016

NOTES

1   Stuart Hall, 'Encoding and Decoding in Television Discourse' in Simon During (ed), *The Cultural Studies Reader*, Taylor & Francis, 1993, p8.

5

The Memory of Hope (2017)
by Aïda Muluneh

Aïda Muluneh exists in a different dimension. She is primarily concerned with bending the old narratives of time back into a brilliant and life-affirming place of different possible futures and knowledge exchanges. Her work constitutes an uneasy but beautiful presence as she brings into focus mythical, majestic beings that call those who destroy hope to account.

Throughout this series, Muluneh makes transformative magic happen. This magic embraces four important features of life: nature, gender, culture and memory. These serene, staged photographs deliberately play with the viewer's sense of place. Every image is a theatrical act of dislocation from a reality that is, for many, increasingly hard to bear.

If there is nothing 'real' throughout this body of work then these images can only come from what lies beyond the eye. The photographs therefore function not as answers to a given condition but as entrypoints to different portals of understanding. They are keys to new chambers and reminders for us that through strong and interconnected memories, hope may not be lost.

These images are made out of a pressing desire to change the viewer's perception of how we act upon and through our time on this planet, spiritually as well as communally. The potent primary colours surrounding, worn by and painted on the women within these frames delinks the subject dramatically from the potentially harsh aspects of the documentary mode. As a collective body of work, they ignite the poetry of time and break its linear drive to consign everything to the past.

To call forth these women here as active agents for change gives them an incredible sense of power. They function as healers and leaders, though purposefully they are surrounded by an air of reluctance. It's as if they may have been among us before, given us the memory of hope before, and now they are as timeless beings, aware that we are not listening. They seem – rightly so – disappointed in much of what we have done with the world. The disruption of time, place and space within this work produces a photographic encounter that addresses a stark reality: something has gone drastically wrong with humanity. The guardians of hope sent forth by Muluneh signpost the way to change, should we stop our accelerated journey long enough to decode the frames.

One of the photographs, *The Mirage of Hope* (2017), typifies the feeling within the series. The subject sits among clouds, eyes closed in contemplative reflection. The work reaffirms the idea that we can also see without looking and that images are always with us, internally and externally. She wears a light, bright blue dress, which is decorated with a lone, red star. It is echoed in colour by a red, origami boat, floating calmly into the image. The presence of the boat signals a childlike innocence and the aspiration to travel. The red star positioned on the dress functions here as a navigational way-finder to a potential better place for all those who are directionless in the vastness of the blue. It's as if the mirage of hope will only appear once the traveller has arrived at a certain point of no return, which may well be death, if the direction or course is not corrected.

Within a mise-en-scéne of melancholy and reflection, this work functions as a profound reminder that hope is fragile and therefore must be sought out and cared for at all times. As a body of work, *The Memory of Hope* series suggests that humans are duty-bound to make sure that hope is kept alive for every generation, and that history as it is currently constituted needs to be rearticulated, reimagined and realigned if the idea of hope or justice is to survive in any real or life-affirming sense.

In the photograph titled *The American Dream* (2017), the horror of lynching is recalled through the presence of a surreal, electric blue rope tied in the form of the Hangman's Knot. The rope, framed in red, cuts across the shadow cast by the woman in the photograph and sits menacingly over the neck. It hovers there with intent, evoking violence, injustice, fear and racial hatred. The ghost-like figure, whose face, neck and hands are painted white, casts her gaze towards the left-hand corner of the frame, inviting the viewer to consider how violence haunts our current condition.

The subject is brought further into focus through a series of black, circular flecks or markings that have been painted onto her neck. These markings work optically to stretch the neck further in the mind's eye, rendering a form of strangulation. They also recall the rows of African bodies represented in the etchings from 1788 of the slave ship, Brooks. These etchings were used by abolitionists to illustrate the horror of human cargo that made up the transatlantic slave trade. *The Memory of Hope* (2017) works then to reawaken the disastrous facts of European colonial violence as directed against the black body. This dark, brutal past is the place where hope is in its most critical condition, as it struggles for survival through history, politics and daily life.

In a final twist with time through this photograph, Muluneh seemingly offers the viewer a gift: a slice of succulent watermelon. The subject carefully holds the fruit up for our scrutiny. The red of the melon sits comfortably within the frame as it echoes the red used to frame the subject's shadow. The melon's black seeds are evident, each of them with the potential to grow into forms of nourishment, with careful nurturing.

However, this offering becomes unsettled by the presence of a black fly on the melon's right-hand edge. It calls forth the company of rot and death into the image, reaffirming for the viewer that many of the good things offered up in the world in the shape of progress have troubled histories. The look of resignation on the subject's face proclaims through this offering that she is indeed one of the 'strange fruits' immortalised in song by Billie Holiday. Muluneh has summoned the ghosts of lynchings past into the now. In doing so, she tells us that if this historical condition gets lost in time, it will continue to be part of our uncomfortable present.

An edited version of this essay first appeared in Foam Magazine *in 2020.*

6

On Wilfred Ukpong

Film and photographic cosmic travellers such as Wilfred Ukpong call forth non-prescriptive, non-linear readings of the past and demand that the kaleidoscopic condition of personal, cultural and national memory is forged into new and different, jazz-like rhythmic formations. Ukpong's visual world is a place of no one direction, no solid state, as in the realm of African cosmologies. Political memory functions and agitates within personal and political space, positioning both the audience and the maker not as subjects fixed in any given moment, but as active, time-bending agents, continuously engaged across different spaces, temporalities and universes. This is where repressed knowledges are free and alive, shared and embraced, and nothing is history as everything that has passed is alive in the present, moulding and reworking our humanity. Within the cosmos of Ukpong's praxis, his otherworldly outsiderism becomes a form of future thinking and being. His subjects function as Time Lords, bringing back and forth that which has been lost, silenced, stolen and overlooked, and part of their transgressive nature involves taking apart the past in the present so as to forge new futures and claim new rights. Here, gods and different beings are rendered not as external and distant but as part of the human, representational, receptive whole. In these external and internal multiverse spaces, to embrace and to love all that which is strange and to treat that which is unfamiliar with respect and hospitality is, by way of being human, an act of restorative, decolonial care.

2020

Human Rights,
Human Wrongs

7

Disposable People:
Contemporary Global Slavery

Roger Malbert: Tell us about the genesis of this project. Was it prompted by the activities in 2007 commemorating the abolition of the slave trade throughout the British Empire?

Mark Sealy: From late 2005 and throughout 2006 there was a lot of what could be described as 'white noise' produced by various cultural and political institutions about the 200th anniversary of the abolition of the slave trade in Britain. Picking up on the frequency of information circulated by many of the UK's major museums regarding plans for public events and the building of new institutions and memorials aimed at commemorating the 1807 Act, it became clear to me that debates about the condition of contemporary global slavery and the continued economic exploitation of people were not being addressed. I objected to the fact that an act of Parliament in 1807 was being flagged up as the defining moment marking the beginning of the end of slavery, as if in one great, British, philanthropic, enlightened moment, African slaves were gifted their freedom.

The national focus on the 1807 Act had the effect of glossing over the political realities and legacy of slavery today. With so much attention focused on anti-slavery campaigners such as William Wilberforce and Thomas Clarkson, what was, in fact, occurring was a form of selective cultural amnesia. The end of slavery was being celebrated as a purely British affair and historicised in a way that positioned Britain as the great liberating force. This meant that other important forms of resistance to slavery were eclipsed or negated – for example, the eighteenth-century revolutionary leader Toussaint L'Ouverture's brilliant military campaigns for freedom, which defeated both the French and British imperial powers and finally led to the establishment of Haiti as the first free black republic. Typically, important campaigns of black resistance to slavery were being rendered insignificant. The battle for freedom that took place on Hispaniola is vital to our understanding of the wider political context that enabled the British government finally to realise that the trading in humans had to end.

Disposable People (2008) is intended to address the here and now, to draw attention to the fact that human trafficking for commercial gain is still a global problem. Now, as in the past, global economic market forces are still the major contributing factor in making human life disposable, and the link between capitalism and slavery remains very active. Today's forced displacement of rural people in the name of progress has echoes of the transatlantic slave trade. This project is, therefore, an invitation to recognise that the wretched conditions of slavery have never really left us. It is an enquiry into how slavery has simply evolved.

I wanted to investigate how the subject of slavery could be addressed explicitly through documentary photography, how its victims could be visualised against the grain of historical representations of slavery. Bearing in mind the recognised limits of documentary photography (and its reputation as not being the innocent carrier of historical truth) this was bound to be a challenge, both curatorially and for the photographers themselves. Addressing the visibility of disenfranchised people has always been a principal concern for Autograph ABP since its very inception over twenty years ago. For two decades, we have been supporting work that unhinges the stereotypes and contests the dominant ideology of Western history. If anything, these concerns will become even more pronounced in the future as the condition of marginalised groups remains a major political issue.

Article Six of the Universal Declaration of Human Rights states: 'Everyone has the right to recognition everywhere as a person before the law.' The histories of photography and the question of black cultural absence are major problems for photography, which until recently has been dominated by a type of image-making that is susceptible to myriad charges of exploitation. I would argue that everyone has the right to recognition everywhere as a person before the law – *and the camera*. The question of cultural authority is a vital

issue that has haunted documentary photography since its invention. I am not sure if these critical questions have been adequately
addressed within postmodern theoretical debates. *Disposable People*
affords us the opportunity to revisit a key issue within photography,
that of representation.

RM: Can we take up the question of documentary photography's
status as a campaigning tool for revealing social reality and implicitly as an instrument for change?

MS: Photography's role as a campaigning tool for highlighting forms
of social injustice has a long historical tradition, for example in the
photographs of Jacob Riis and the Farm Security Administration
programmes.[1] Later, the work of contemporary theorists and artists
like John Tagg, Martha Rosler and Abigail Solomon-Godeau
deconstructed the documentary photograph, revealing it to be not
simply the bearer of a given truth. One of the aims of this project
is to provide a platform for re-examining some key issues relating
to documentary photography – namely, how to represent without
exploiting, and whether it is indeed possible to represent a subject's
condition in the full knowledge that a photograph is not produced
in a political or cultural vacuum. Worthy images of the disenfranchised do several things at once: they make us aware of the tragic
circumstances in which people live and they remind us of the victim's
helplessness while affirming our own sense of security and power.

RM: There is the obvious problem of information overload. When
TV and video permeate visual culture and every mobile phone
contains a camera, the traditional role of the photojournalist is surely
diminished, if a part of that is to witness, to bring to light unseen
and unknown realities. And, in a digital age, we can no longer trust
the photograph to provide an authentic record.

MS: The notion of image overload is an important issue, and the
impact of the digital revolution on the Western world is profound.
It is clear that the ease of transmission of photographs is now very
different; images appear to leak from places they are not supposed
to, which makes them even more compelling or repulsive.

But when we think about mass access to the production and distribution of images in a global context, we need to remember that, for example, in December 2007, internet users in Africa constituted only 3.4 per cent of total worldwide web users.[2] The majority of the world's population does not have access to cameras or the internet. Therefore, we could say that the traditional role of the socially committed photojournalist has not diminished, it has simply changed in relation to how the West consumes and produces images.

RM: The realities represented in these images are inflected in all kinds of ways, they are not simply objective reportage. They are framed firstly by the pictorial and journalistic conventions of the age, and secondly they are filtered through the consciousness of the photographer. All the photographers in *Disposable People* are creative individuals whose sensibilities are evident in almost every picture they take. In this sense, they are artists; although they may also be journalists and activists. In the context of contemporary art, there are questions to consider about the relationship between the ethical (or political) and the aesthetic dimensions, particularly today when social documentary modes are often adopted as a strategy by artists whose purpose is less to reveal reality than to create a powerful, highly-charged image. The primary aim of the socially aware documentary photographer is surely to bring reality home; yet many of their images are aesthetically satisfying, beautifully composed and so on. But what does that mean for the viewer? How does the moral urgency, the imperative to act, get transmitted? Or is it really that the role of activist is assigned to the photographer, while the viewer remains a passive, disinterested onlooker?

MS: The problem for documentary photography is that it is now increasingly clear that the viewers are not prepared to consume the photograph with the same emphatic blind faith as in the past. As the artist and cultural theorist Abigail Solomon-Godeau reminds us in her essay 'Who Is Speaking Thus? Some Questions about Documentary Photography': 'The Photographer's desire to build pathos or sympathy into the image, to invest the subject with either an emblematic or an archetypal importance, to visually dignify labour or poverty, is a problem to the extent that such strategies eclipse or obscure the political sphere whose determinations, actions, and instruments are not in themselves visual.'[3] Therefore, and with the above quotation in mind, it is not surprising that when we come to think about the image of contemporary slavery, it is often difficult to visualise the political conditions that bind the victims; in many instances they are lost in the text. The challenge for these photographers was to make visible what is concealed.

RM: Whatever one thinks of the proposition that the photographer's sympathy actually obscures the underlying political and economic reality, it is certainly true that the visual alone cannot convey it. That is why the images here are not treated as autonomous, but require text to explain the situations depicted. And the photographers have all presented their images in narrative sequence; this too deflects from the aestheticising impulse.

   In discussing the split or tension between the ethical and the aesthetic dimensions of documentary photography, Martha Rosler distinguishes usefully between production and consumption. She writes of 'the well-entrenched paradigm in which the documentary image has two moments: the "immediate" instrumental one, in which an image is caught or created out of the stream of the present and held up as testimony ... and the conventional "aesthetic-historical" moment, less indefinable in its boundaries, in which the viewer's argumentativeness cedes to the ... pleasure afforded by the aesthetic "rightness" ... of the image.'[4] It could be asked why we need images of such profound or subtle beauty to make us aware of injustice? Is the sympathy of the photographer essential to the power of the photograph? You chose to work on this project with socially committed photojournalists rather than with artists using documentary modes. Will you say something about how you see the relation between documentary photography and contemporary art?

MS: Working with socially committed photographers who are grounded in the tradition of the documentary allowed us to move away from the idea that contemporary global slavery could be treated as an 'artist in residence'-type project that would end up saying more about the artist than the social conditions in focus. I wanted to work with photographers who actively engage in providing documentary stories for editorial circulation. That is a very specific form of visual intervention. When done well, the documentary photograph is not just in the news, it *is* the news.

RM: On the question of how much an image reveals and what it conceals, it is striking that many of the images in *Disposable People* are quiet and understated by the standards of international photojournalism. We are quite used to seeing photographs of carnage and destruction. We know how to look and look away. Most of the photographs here show ordinary people going about their everyday lives, and if the underlying reality is violent exploitation and a criminal abuse of human rights, it is not always immediately apparent. This is very much the world as we know it.

MS: The latent and less obvious violence within photography is an issue that is hardly discussed. In many instances, photojournalists who desire to get close to the carnage and destruction of an area of tragedy adopt a dualistic position in terms of how the subject is presented. The victim is often identified and represented in rather simplistic terms. The point here is that much of the visual violence we are subjected to functions in a similar way to rumour. Somehow the origins of the situation are never made apparent but the results can be lethal. The codes of how photojournalism renders the victim have become internationally standardised. The victim becomes a universal 'Other'. Therefore, photographers working within a conflict or disaster zone repeatedly fall into an inherent trap of trying to present a sense of horror in order to provoke in the viewer a humanitarian response – which is often momentary, persisting only until we turn away or turn the page.

Good intentions are not a guarantee of the work a photograph eventually ends up doing. Often the more covert forms of violence contained within a photograph are quickly legitimised because of the obvious or direct 'good' work the image does for the reader. The image's undercurrents also need to be examined. Is it enough to reproduce yet another image of an African child dying with flies in their eyes? The primary function of a stereotypical image of famine is produced with a particular aim in mind or a prize in sight. This form of image-making is therefore justified because of the results it yields, or the causes it highlights. The fact that many of these images perform acts of erasure is denied. Aid agencies are particularly susceptible to this problem. Therefore, if we have conditions where the visual exploitation of people is accepted as long as it is for a good cause, we have a condition where certain sections of humanity will always be rendered pathetic. So as far as photography is concerned, we have a condition where the meanings within a photograph become difficult to fix. The 'punctum' ('that which pierces the viewer'), which Roland Barthes famously refers to, fails to function.[5] The violent nature of images gets absorbed into the violence of the everyday. The strength of this project lies in the fact that many of the photographs included in *Disposable People* are not remarkably dramatic; they are quiet and contemplative. They could be described as everyday moments in the lives of those who have experienced one of the most insidious forms of violence: to be made both invisible and disposable.

This interview first appeared in the publication Documenting Disposable People: Contemporary Global Slavery (*Hayward Gallery 2008), which accompanied an exhibition organised by Autograph and Hayward Touring. The exhibition,* Disposable People, *took an in-depth look at the prevalence of global slavery in the twenty-first century through the lenses of eight, internationally acclaimed Magnum photographers. It began at the Royal Festival Hall in London and toured to venues across the UK.*

NOTES

1 Abigail Solomon-Godeau, *Photography at the Dock: Essays on Photographic History, Institutions, and Practices*, University of Minnesota Press: Minneapolis, 2003.

2 www.internetworldstats.com/stats1.htm.

3 Solomon-Godeau, *op. cit.*, p179.

4 Martha Rosler, 'In, Around and Afterthoughts (On Documentary Photography)' in *martha rosler, 3 works*, Press of the Nova Scotia College of Art & Design, 2006, p81.

5 Roland Barthes, *Camera Lucida*, Richard Howard (trans), Noonday Press: New York, 1981.

8

Beyond the Lens

It was not until 1993 that the General Assembly of the United Nations finally adopted the Declaration on the Elimination of Violence against Women. Article One reads:

> For the purposes of this Declaration, the term 'violence against women' means any act of gender-based violence that results in, or is likely to result in, physical, sexual or psychological harm or suffering to women, including threats of such acts, coercion or arbitrary deprivation of liberty, whether occurring in public or in private life.[1]

For centuries human trafficking has been a lucrative business. It is currently estimated to have a market value of over 32 billion US dollars. Forced prostitution of women is the most widespread form of human trafficking today. According to Professor Kevin Bales, the world's leading expert on contemporary global slavery, poverty, deprivation, the desire for a better life and the need to escape conflict and oppression are all vital elements that bring people into contact with traffickers.[2] Deception and false promises are important strategies employed by traffickers. Gaining the confidence of the targeted individuals and their families is an essential part of the trafficking process.

For the victim, hope turns to tragedy once transportation begins. Kevin Bales states: 'To be without documents while in transit is to be placed immediately in the control of the trafficker.'[3] The dispossession of identity is the first major act of violence aimed at the victim. Stripping away the subject's identity prepares the ground for the subject to become a non-citizen, a person without rights or protection. It's an act of violence that has similar echoes across the historical application of photography when focused on the Other. 'The aim of the trafficker will be to disorientate the victim, to increase his or her dependence, to establish fear and obedience, to gain control.'[4] The more they resist, the greater the brutality, until – like most slaves – their will to resist is finally crushed. The journey towards a hopeful future quickly turns into a journey of utter despair, violent degradation and possible death. The key question of what happens to an individual once the traffickers have no value for them is rarely considered. Over time, the value of human life has decreased; the more people attempt to escape poverty and conflict, the easier it is to exploit them.

Photography as a medium is most suited to forms of documentary commentary and has historically been used to portray, frame and display people in both their most glorious and most debased conditions. Theoretical debates on photography are racked with issues concerning photography's 'indexical aspect, which comes from the fact that since a photograph results from exposure to a pre-existing entity, it directly bears the entity's imprint and can therefore supply evidence about the object it depicts'.[5] The production of photographic evidence opens up questions concerning power and post/colonial ways of knowing, which link to debates around state control over the individual, crime, punishment and societal classification, in addition to the nature of Western 'scopic' power.[6]

The photographs from Dana Popa's series *Not Natasha* (2009) perform several tasks. As a body of documentary photographs, they serve as a reminder of the wide-reaching effects of human trafficking on the individual subject, the victim. Popa's photographs work primarily within the classic tradition of the documentary genre, where 'causality is vague, blame is not assigned, fate cannot be overcome.'[7] Her use of colour is a deliberate turn away from the gritty and distant realism associated with black-and-white documentary photography. Colour brings the viewer closer to the victim, effectively closing the distance between them and us.

Popa's photographs are an enquiry into an acute and pervasive form of violence against women. The loss and absence portrayed in Popa's photographs – which often depict empty domestic spaces – resonate with the violence associated with forms of cultural erasure in which names are changed, histories are rewritten and deep-rooted societal relationships are severed. Popa's photographs are a tragic reminder of just how vulnerable and powerless women are globally, and the absence displayed exposes the futility of universal declarations like the one at the beginning of this essay. Popa's photographs act as metaphorical markers on the social conditions across cultures that have served to lock women into forms of servitude for men.

In an additional cruel, visual twist, Popa invites us to recognise the other form of violence that is at play throughout this work: the ongoing misery of those who have been left behind to wait, in the hope that one day the loved one will return home. The portraits of those who can only wait and the photographs they cling to of those who have been trafficked become tragic icons of hope, as the person who has departed will never again fit the image that is held up for us to observe.

The psychological damage inflicted on those who have managed to return home is beyond the spectacle of any one photograph. The photographic image in this instance cannot carry the burden of personal experience. Popa represents the women who return home through a veiled sense of shame; their identities have to be altered for the sake of their own protection.

Popa's extensive project, which took several years to make, attempts to address the wider impact that human trafficking has on the family and extended social relations. The photographs serve to memorialise those who have vanished. They also operate as tools of testimony for those who have returned. As documents, the photographs prove nothing. Instead they act as signifiers of emptiness, waiting, emotional damage and external harm. Within this body of photographs, the doctrine of a decisive photographic moment is abandoned, and what is revealed is the importance of time exchanged between the photographer and the subject. There is no critical moment of entrapment or release relating to the subject in focus. These photographs offer no reprieve from the violence experienced by these women and their families. The interiority of the photographic work – the empty rooms, the dark and claustrophobic spaces – portray a chronic condition of despair and highlight the conditions that make it possible for human trafficking to thrive. Popa's investment in the subject is therefore beyond the lens. Her photographs operate as markers of her intention to take action and responsibility.

Catastrophe, as it is usually understood emerges, erupting as an event, sharply drawing the line between before and after, manufacturing its emergence as a riddle: how and why is this happening? Why now? Why in this manner? What to do about catastrophe requires exhaustive research that could bring to the surface more and more facts to explain its eventuation. But the verge of catastrophe, does not emerge, it is not exactly an event, and has no power to create a difference. It exists on the surface, completely open to the gaze and yet evading it, because there is nothing to distinguish it from the surroundings in which it exists.[8]

Popa's photographic project focuses on two distinctive, visual forms of violence that should not be separated from each other: the violence of poverty and the violence of exploitation. By focusing on domestic interiors, Popa signifies to her audience that it is not enough to simply talk about the actual victim of trafficking, that it is not enough to highlight how the victims have been abused and the personal torment they have suffered both mentally and physically. None of this makes sense unless we take time to analyse the cultural and economic conditions that make it possible for women's lives to be seen only in terms of their potential for exploitation.

Documentary photography has, in many regards, taken a theoretical battering over the last few decades. However, in a celebrity-obsessed, globalised world, the real value of documentary photography is that it reminds us of our privileges. Seen as a relational tool, it will always tell us as much about ourselves as it does about the subject in focus.

This text first appeared in Foam Magazine, *Issue 18, in 2009.*

NOTES

1 United Nations Human Rights, Office of the High Commissioner, 'Declaration on the Elimination of Violence Against Women', www.ohchr.org/en/professionalinterest/pages/violenceagainstwomen.aspx, 20 December 1993.

2 Kevin Bales, *Understanding Global Slavery*, University of California Press: Berkeley, 2005, p145.

3 *Ibid.*

4 *Ibid.*, p141.

5 Tom Gunning, 'Tracing the Individual Body: Photography, Detection, and early Cinema', in Leo Charney and Vanessa R. Schwartz (eds), *Cinema and the invention of Modern Life,* University of California Press: Berkeley, 1995, p20.

6 Allen Feldman, 'Violence and Vision: The prosthetics and aesthetics of terror', in Fernando Coronil and Julie Skurski (eds), *States of Violence,* University of Michigan Press: Ann Arbor, 2006, pp425-468.

7 Martha Rosler, *3 works,* The Press of Nova Scotia College of Art and Design: Halifax, 2006, p76.

8 Ariella Azoulay, *The Civil Contract of Photography,* Zone Books: New York, 2008, p291.

9

The Event in Focus Is (not) Over

What would happen if we finally realised that what we are looking for in photographs cannot be seen or described but must be felt? What if we understood that it is through our affect that we can appreciate the complexity of our contemporary being, and that for a photograph to have any real meaning, it must be able to move us in a unique way? It would follow that we must unlearn any universal ideas about what knowledge an image may contain.

Photographs are slippery objects. They keep past events alive, they prevent closure and they haunt the now. They manage time in the present; each time we come to read a photograph, our moment in time is shifted. Photographs can pull the viewer back and forth through time. They remind us of the way we were since we are different upon every viewing. Photographs call on memories that are both real and imagined. Viewing a photograph is like receiving an invitation from time and space to walk through an emotional, cultural or political portal where our own identity is made heavier by the gravity of past events. Photographs can also help us to think about a future tense – where we might want to be – and give us the chance to move beyond where we once were.

Once we pass through the portal, the photograph becomes consigned to a place in memory, and memory is a place where our time – past, present and future – is held captive. Painful parts of memory often get locked away, too difficult to deal with in the present, unless the event in focus is not over. If it has no decisive end, it becomes a living thing that can't be framed, dissolved or disappeared. It acts on the body like an overbearing historical weight that moves in culture under the cloak of denial and disavowal, unable to be touched but nevertheless intensely felt – an ever-present colonial now. It pulls the present and future towards its own violent, homogenising black hole. Some have no choice but to feel the past as well as see it.

For Délio Jasse, the events of violent colonial time cannot be allowed to fade conveniently into the narrative of Eurocentric political histories and epistemes. That would be an injustice to the global majority of formerly colonised peoples. Jasse's work brings moments of colonial denial back into focus and it is here that he proclaims that we all have a moral duty not to forget. This is a process that exposes and critiques the dominant narratives of colonial history which have devoured so much of the story of the world. The result is that many human lives and cultures have systematically been erased from time. This makes the work of unpicking and remaking the world's archives an essential part of rebuilding a pluriversal story for humanity. That, in many ways, is at the heart of the radical turn Délio Jasse is making in, on and with photography.

Jasse's work, which is integral to his experience of being, finds him compelled to search amongst discarded moments of a people's lives, especially those who have dwelled within the constructed comfort of their sense of superiority, luxury and privilege. Jasse's art recycles the colonial moments that lie among the ruins, in the basements and in the cracks of the violent spaces of our time. These violent spaces can be found in the archives of museums and places of learning throughout the Western world. The task now is to reinterpret these archives so that the nature of their violence can be read.

His images form an important part of a long-standing grievance procedure by all those who have endured imperial violence. This grievance lies deep within the liberated anti-colonial mind, best articulated by Frantz Fanon in his seminal text, *Black Skin, White Masks*, which demands justice and recognition for colonised peoples. Jasse deploys various printing methods, both old and new, to highlight how time is concealed within his praxis. He reanimates unwanted photographic corpses and reproductive tools that have in the past been put to service of othering human subjects, transforming them into new objects of inquiry. They do the necessary and unsettling visual work of throwing new light onto the residue of colonial presences that seep out into our everyday.

Jasse's work in the macro- and micro-events of colonial time serve to excavate uncomfortable pasts, and his body of work functions as a visual signpost to the way 'they' – the colonised Others – were. His images make manifest the dark colonial architectures of knowledge that dominate our worlds, and the moments he brings into focus remind us that colonialism was built on strategies of extermination and extraction.

Jasse's series *Nova Lisboa* (2018), for example, is laced with a sense of foreboding. It signals the coloniser's privilege, arrogance and cultural dominance. One work from the series warrants particular attention. It's a full-length portrait of a European man, smart but casually dressed in a shirt, jacket and trousers. He stands on the pavement of a wide, tree-lined street, confidently posing, with his left hand placed in his pocket. He faces the photographer directly and his expression carries a slight smile back to the camera.

It's a sunny day in Nova Lisboa. The colonial city is always home being made elsewhere, at the expense of the Other. On the right-hand side of the image, we can see a series of chairs placed in the street that suggest the presence of a café or bar that our subject may have been visiting. Behind the man, we can observe more Europeans either about to enter buildings or simply engaged in conversation on the street. The mise-en-scéne of the image suggests a relaxed moment across Nova Lisboa. The parked cars and the bicycle leaning against the wall of a building work towards completing an image of colonial content.

However, the photograph carries within it a distinctive charge that draws the viewer away from the central character. To the left of the image, a young, black boy is present. He wears short trousers, a shirt and no shoes. His presence is in complete contrast to the central figure of the middle-aged European man. His stride seems relaxed and confident as he, in turn, observes the photographer observing the intended subject. Here it's as if the boy has defiantly emerged out of the body of the European subject to disrupt the self-assured moment being framed.

Situated in the background, the boy's presence at the time of photograph being taken makes him merely part of the architecture of the scene. But in the now, the presence of the boy makes the event of this photograph something that is not over. His look and presence carry us from the moment of the photograph to this future place, where we too can observe the coloniser affirming his self-image. The boy watching the making of a colonial photographic moment and his presence on the scene become a form of time-turbulence across the image. This is echoed by the use of a green, diagonal, stamp-like text that runs across the image as if it were processed for some form of quality control or classification, two trademark tools of colonial subjugation.

In the image, the boy is moving to a different rhythm to all that surrounds him. His presence is an intrusion across this colonial ideal in the making. What he will come to witness in the future becomes the lens through which we read the scene in the present. Angola, not long after this photograph was taken, became consumed by the theatre of the Cold War, with devastating consequences.

The bodies of work produced by Jasse help us to move towards delinking from the diseases and injustice many of us live with in colonial time. This is because 'from the moment you realize that what seems to be reality, objectivity, and truth is nothing but a hegemonic option, you are already stepping out and inhabiting the decolonial or other liberating options.'[1] Jasse's praxis represents an offer to enter a new time-frame for living and new terms of thinking, to help open up spaces in which we the audience can imagine a more diverse collective visual past, one that acknowledges the injustices wrought by colonial violence.

'The Event in Focus' was commissioned for doc! photo magazine *#46 (2020) by guest editor Daria Tuminas, curator of FOTODOK. The issue was dedicated to the subject of collective memory, and featured artists presented at FOTODOK's exhibition* Joint Memory: Photographic Fragments *(14 November 2019 – 23 February 2020), including Délio Jasse.*

NOTES

1   Walter D. Mignolo and Catherine E. Walsh, *On Decoloniality: Concepts, Analytics, Praxis*, Duke University Press: Durham, 2019, p224.

10

Notes on *Towards a Promised Land* (2005-06), by Wendy Ewald

Photography's past may ultimately become the place where we begin to understand our deepest human failings. Conferred a sense of greatness throughout its history, photography is burdened with poignancies, regret and moments of disrespect concerning the human condition. We now have to consider with urgency what its future entails, who speaks to it, through it and with it.

Meaningful collaborations within photography allow for building places of care rather than capture. We need to peel back the problematic archival skin to begin restorative dialogues across photography's multiple sites of internal bleeding. Creating places of recognition, equality and understanding within photography means that we can work on or cure its spectacular, dehumanising, violent addictions. Each truly collaborative exchange within photography is an act of liberation, knowledge exchange, respect and generosity, possible only through mutual recognition, closeness and trust. When engaging in a collaborative moment, everything is gravity. A new space of meaning is born where strength and vulnerability converge with grace and dynamic force. The hollow of 'not knowing' can then become an exciting proposition, a new adventure.

Throughout her long and considered photographic career, Wendy Ewald has collaborated with marginalised people. The meanings produced through her photographs, combined with the testimonies of her subjects, generate profound understandings of human emotions and relationships beyond the act of photographing. The process of making images in partnership with the subject is essential to Ewald. Her photographic encounters, especially those with children, help us see each other more clearly, through dark, uncertain and alienating times.

Consider, then, Ewald's large scale, black-and-white portraits of children mounted on the seaside cliffs of Margate, the disused amusement park, Dreamland, and different sites across the town centre in 2006. Effectively, what was presented worked on the viewer as trusted offerings, especially to those who refuse to recognise the refugee or displaced child as human. Uryi, a young boy of around ten from Grodno, Belarus, had his portrait placed on the towering brickwork that formed part of the old Dreamland amusement park complex. His presence high above the town, staring directly down on the audience, operated as a direct provocation concerning the development of societal futures. Uryi's portrait prominently positioned on the Dreamland site prompts critical questions about how and why this child's image is presented here. As a place of amusement, Dreamland once fuelled the imagination of both the young and old, and Uryi's presence on the building stokes thoughts of escape from the everyday. However, Uryi's facial expression does not signal that he is involved in pleasurable activities. On the contrary, his stoic, enquiring gaze suggests that he is absorbed in a state of reflection. The text embedded within the photograph reinforces our potential understanding of his condition. It reads: 'It happened that we had to leave our lovely city.' These simple, polite, handwritten words that scroll up the left-hand side of Uryi's portrait and arc over his head inform the viewer that all is not well, and that Uryi may be both internally and geographically dislocated.

In viewing the portrait of Uryi, other texts of dislocation were also present, operating outside of the image but close to it. The fading words 'Dreamland' frame Uryi vertically and horizontally, fixing him forever in a space where pleasure, hopes and dreams have become washed-out states, not quite vanished but clearly on the verge of disappearance. As words and as remains of corporate branding, these tired advertising signs announcing Dreamland are also embedded into the fabric of the building.

Uryi's portrait located on Dreamland's tower played an emotional and slippery game with the viewer. On the one hand, the image offered the audience a sense of new possible futures and a place of refuge, thus keeping the idea of a dream land alive. However, the photograph simultaneously evokes an insular past, a decaying local nostalgia dead in the present, as Dreamland falls in disrepair. The portrait of Uryi then expands beyond him and opens space for conversations regarding the conditions in English seaside towns and the politics of state disinvestment.

Ewald's portraits of young people that have newly arrived in Margate unsettle the status quo of the environment. These young people will always be from elsewhere. The underlying tension that runs through this project doesn't rest solely with the difficult experiences the children shared with the audiences; this work also brings into focus questions of hospitality, burden and care, since the viewers who look into their eyes daily as they move through the town have to consider what it truly means to welcome a stranger in such harsh social circumstances. *Towards a Promised Land* (2005-06) as a photographic collaboration calls forth the idea of shared journeys, both physical and psychological, highlighting the never-ending processes of humans requesting recognition, both from other individuals and from states.

Ewald's portrait of a child named Reza was positioned on Margate's concrete 'protective' seawall. In spending time with the image, the eye is drawn to the multiple transition points visible in his face. Wispy facial hair suggests a process of thickening, as if his body's journey to maturity is burying the Reza in his own eyes. His eyebrows reach for each other in slow but progressive growth. His top lip is shadowed by the presence of fine dark hair, signalling that, visually, his childhood will soon be over. His eyes are slightly puffed and wrinkled, on the edge of adolescence, possibly due to sleepless nights. Reza stares back, stoic and vulnerable, resistant and hopeful. However, it is the text he chooses to share with us that anchors him to our hearts. Arching over Reza's head from shoulder to shoulder and working as a textual frame within the image are the words 'I am mourning that I don't have my mother with me and her protecting shadow over my head'.

The deployment of the texts within these images operates as a form of testimony or confession. They assist the work the images do by inviting the viewer to move beyond the comfortable state of cultural and consumer empathy. The uncomfortable aspect of a project like *Towards a Promised Land* is that, as a set of images, words and placements, it pushes the encounter, the seeing moment of the photograph, towards a place of ethical looking.

2021

11

The Canvases of Representation and the Photographs of Nontsikelelo Veleko

In time, we shall be in a position to bestow on South Africa the greatest possible gift – a more human face.

Steve Biko, *I Write What I Like*

I t's now evident that curatorial work in the field of photography across the continent of Africa has, especially in the last twenty years or so, produced some intriguing interpretations of what constitutes good 'African photography'. Some exhibitions have been truly innovative and in time have proved to be historically important moments. *Africa Explores: 20th Century African Art*, New York, 1991; *24th Rencontres Internationales de la Photographie*, Arles, 1993; and the first *Rencontres de Bamako* in 1994 were exceptional moments in the presentation of contemporary African photography. It is true that many exhibitions have done good work in allowing audiences to discover African photographers, but others have served only to expose a deep-seated, conservative approach to contextualising, presenting and exploiting the complex nature of photography produced by indigenous African photographers.

An obvious and recent example of an inherently conservative approach to working with African photographers was the restaging in March 2005 of Samuel Fosso's photograph *Le Chef* as a live performance, which saw the artist himself displayed in the main shop window of one of London's most fashionable department stores, Selfridges, on Oxford Street. This event, though satirical in nature, not only restaged one of Fosso's most celebrated photographs but also recreated the violence of colonial capture, display and invention of the African subject. Fosso's ill-conceived project menacingly echoed the large-scale temporary events that took place at the Great Exhibitions held in cosmopolitan centres such Paris and London at the turn of the nineteenth century. These events saw the colonised subjects of imperial Europe put on display for the entertainment of millions of Europeans in a form of cultural ridicule.

When dealing with African cultures in Europe, one has to be critically aware of the impact that these historically and culturally biased encounters have had on our understanding of Africa. If Europe insists on inventing Africa for popular Eurocentric consumption then those of us who are now working with images from Africa should be asking what the cultural purpose our work is. Africa, with a landmass that covers over twenty per cent of the total land area of the earth, including over fifty countries that contain a myriad of different cultural formations seamlessly sliding across borders, cannot possibly be reduced to, or framed as, one historical moment, one big idea. The very idea of 'an African photography' is thus a deeply problematic conception that needs unravelling and rethinking.

There is no doubt that a rich photographic tradition has existed across the continent since the invention of the medium. We must therefore recognise that the history of photography on the continent of Africa has not yet been fully written, especially while it continues to be presented as an adjunct of the medium's growth.

This continued invention of Africa in Europe is a recurring cultural nightmare. It perpetuates an undercurrent of desire that forces us to keep Africa at a distance. The danger of a continued cultural distancing brought on by objectifying the African subject affects our capacity in Europe to engage with, and respond to, the humanity of the African Other. Each time we objectify the African body it reignites the historical horror of African anonymity, cultural erasure and the fantastic inventions of our own imaginary Africa.

Observing how African photography has been pulled from the margins towards the cultural centre is an interesting exercise in postcolonial engagement that resonates with the funk of cultural imperialism and the aesthetic management of the Other. The legal actions over 'Who Owns Seydou Keïeta' that saw two European collectors fighting in court over 'ownership' of Seydou Keïta's archive and prints in 2006[1] and the Golden Lion award for Malick Sidibé at the Venice Biennale in 2007 are contrasting, defining moments in the history of photography and on the landscape of Western visual culture. Both situations raise questions about the place of African photography, its position within the art market, the construction of canonical figures, the intentionality of the photographer and, critically, the reception of an image once removed from its original field of perception, reception and use.

The tension of representational politics, even if one desires not to be caught within these frames of reference, simply won't go away, especially when photographic works produced by artists in Africa are judged from the perspective of European, ethnocentric, institutional concerns. At present, African photography can be read as an impossible science. Its meaning is always open to re-invention. The globalisation process of African visual culture through the international museum and art gallery networks has the capacity to render local concerns – the specific moments of interest or nuances of expression – invisible, lost in translation. Large group shows that collect and display African artists are clearly susceptible to reconstructing an experience that is not unlike the cultural work that was done by the Great Exhibitions of the late nineteenth and early twentieth centuries.

The current size and scale of museums in the West, as they increase in capacity and compete for globally trans-fluid audiences, are seriously in danger of turning the art-object encounter into a theme-park experience in which the role of curator functions like that of the circus ringmaster. This was certainly the case for the last big African art fair in London, part of which was *Africa Remix*, an exhibition that featured more than sixty artists from twenty-five countries. Jonathan Jones, the *Guardian* art critic, gave up trying to present criticism of the work for fear of causing offence, 'In the end, this is a subject I probably shouldn't even be writing about. What do I know? Racism is limitless.'[2] Jones's position is interesting, as it's a clear example of critical judgment being suspended by the overbearing weight of trying to read individual artist's works through the prism of an incredibly diverse, geo-politically complex continent.

The reception of African photography is shrouded in discursive debates concerning African modernity, 'and with it a great number of current paradigmatic oppositions have developed: traditional versus modern; oral versus written and printed; agrarian and customary communities versus urban and industrialized civilization; subsistence economies versus highly productive economies',[3] exotic versus violent; famine versus war; and local versus global. Cyclical debates concerning African modernity have become the norm through which we read the art produced across Africa. The quest for the Afro-modern moment or the proof of Afro-cosmopolitanism says more about us in Europe than it does about the subject in focus.

Naturally, the institutional rise of Orientalism must – at least in England and France – be associated with the huge expansion of colonialism and other forms of domination over Asia and Africa taking place at the same time. Not only was a systematic understanding of non-European peoples and their spoken languages needed to control these peoples but a knowledge of their civilizations, by seizing and categorizing their cultures, ensured that the natives themselves could only learn about their own civilizations only through European scholarship'.[4]

It is through the prism of these debates that the photographs of Nontsikelelo Veleko must perform their epistemological work. Her photographs have to rub against the grain of historical visual knowledge concerning how Africa, and in particular South Africa, has been systematically constructed for Eurocentric consumption over time. Her photographs have to work against the historical theoretical inventions of an imagined Africa. This invented Africa has created a fantastic, temporally distant and pessimistic African vision that has come to dominate how and when we see the African subject today.

Veleko's photography turns away from the tradition of Afro-pessimistic history so prevalent in turbulent or melancholic visualizations of African societies. Her work is an active engagement with the now-generation of fashionable people who are not throbbing with the hangover of apartheid. Her found-subjects demand to be considered as subjects living in the moment, a claim common across the world's youth cultures.

Veleko's work oscillates between several photographic traditions. It embraces the style of photography made popular by magazines in the UK such as *Dazed & Confused* and *i-D Magazine*, magazines in which street fashion is the dominant semiotic register. Veleko's models serve as representatives of a people with a shared social formation and cultural identity, who aspire to be identified beyond mere categories. The subjects' desire is to be seen and their willingness to be photographed offers readers of these photographs a visual comment on the post-apartheid condition at work, a condition that isn't trapped by despair and dysfunctional political parties.

In this context, as in all fashion photography, there is a sense of contemporary social anthropology at work in which the more exotic figures and moments are brought into focus for visual pleasure. The point being made by Veleko here is that these individual forms of expression, through fashion, lay claim to a new kind of assertive cultural pattern that reclaims the street in a manner more akin to the historical and political exuberance of black dandyism in Harlem in the 1920s, a moment in history that represented a growing social confidence and new forms of black self-invention.

As Henry Louis Gates aptly demonstrated, 'Negroes are called or call themselves new at what might be considered moments of crisis or times of strange, interesting, and often arresting opportunity. Used to describe an African recently arrived in eighteenth-century England, a newly emancipated slave in the 1870s, or variably, a political radical or poet in the Harlem of the 1920s, the term "new Negro" carries with it an eighteenth- century vision of utopia with a nineteenth-century idea of progress to form a black end-of-the-century dream of an unbroken, unhabituated, neological self.'[5]

But we would be mistaken to read Veleko's photography as simply a meditation on the current state of street fashion in Johannesburg. Having studied at the Market Photo Workshop, a centre that 'has played a pivotal role in the training and growth of South Africa's photographers, ensuring that visual literacy reaches neglected and marginalized parts of our society',[6] it's not surprising that there is a latent sense of political urgency and defiance about her work that wants to look forward into a place of unhinged freedoms. To be really free, one has to have the capacity to imagine or explore what one's life is actually like, not be told what one's place is and not be held or fixed within a scopic regime[7] over which one has no control. The camera, in the hands of Veleko, is really a simple tool with which to carry out the investigations of a life without boundaries, categorisations and obsessions with race. Like Harlem in the 1920s, the subjects of Veleko's photographs are 'not only emphasizing their differences in the way they look and move, but also insist that they have a right to the streets and that the milestones in their collective past are part of the city's history.'[8] Veleko's portraits are therefore a mighty step towards the gift anti-apartheid activist Steve Biko dared to imagine in 1978, the year after Veleko was born: the gift of a new and human face for South Africa.

This article was first published in Foam Magazine No. 23 *on 17 June 2010.*

NOTES

1 Michael Rips, 'Who Owns Seydou Keïta?', www.nytimes.com, 22 January 2006.

2 Jonathan Jones, 'Africa Calling', https://www.theguardian.com/arts/critic/review/0,,1409077,00.html, 9 February 2005.

3 V. Y. Mudimbe, *The Invention of Africa*, Indiana University Press: Bloomington and Indianapolis, 1988, p4.

4 Martin Bernal, *Black Athena: The Afroasiatic Roots of Classical Civilization, Volume 1: The Fabrication of Ancient Greece, 1785-1985*, Rutgers University Press: New Brunswick, 2006, p236.

5 Monica L. Miller, *Slaves to Fashion: Black Dandyism and the Styling of Black Diasporic Identity*, Duke University Durham, 2009, p181.

6 See www.marketphotoworkshop.co.za.

7 The term 'scopic regime' has been defined as 'an ensemble of practices and discourses that establish truth claims, typicality, and credibility of visual acts and objects and politically correct modes of seeing'. Kyle Grayson and Jocelyn Mawdsley, 'Scopic regimes and the visual turn in International Relations: Seeing world politics through the drone', *European Journal of International Relations*, Vol. 25, No. 2, 2019, pp431–457.

8 Miller, *op. cit.*, p199.

12

Label Cultural Baggage

This essay first appeared in the book Hotel Afrique *by Stuart Franklin (Dewi Lewis Publishing 2007). The text is an attempt to locate the historical and cultural context of Franklin's depiction of contemporary Africa as place where power is accommodated through service and luxury; where old colonial legacies and hangovers are played out through expectations of exuberance and privilege, made possible now through global capitalism and political corruption rather than old forms of imperial power.*

It's hard to imagine a discussion about Africa without Europe being part of the equation. The two continents have been in a constant flux and negotiation since time immemorial. However, the Enlightened European thinker conveniently forgot to recognise the inhuman and genocidal nature of Europe's exchanges with Africa. The dark side of European progress, the slave trade, provided much of the human resources necessary for Europe's development into a full-scale economic and military power. It is estimated that 15 million people were forcibly removed from Africa to fuel Western capitalist aspirations.

The Berlin Conference of November 1884-5 was to be the defining moment in the 'Scramble for Africa'. The 'formal' regulation of European domination over the entire continent was being carved out. For three months Europe haggled over establishing geometric boundaries within the interior of the continent, negating the cultural and linguistic boundaries of the indigenous African populations. The misrepresentation of Africa's indigenous cultures as backward and savage is a defining marker of the colonial presence, a literary and visual legacy that has become part of the dominant ideological Western construction of Africa and its peoples today. As one critical observer writes:

> Amongst your characters you must always include the The
> Starving African, who wanders the refugee camp nearly naked,
> and waits for the benevolence of the West. Her children have
> flies on their eyelids and pot bellies, and her breasts are flat and
> empty. She can have no past, no history, such diversions ruin
> the dramatic moment.[1]

The hotel, by definition, has always been a site of privilege, a space
where one is greeted by reception and hopefully a secure welcome,
where one expects service. The status of where you stay and how
you travel – first class, five star, business class or standard class –
has obvious echoes of colonial regimes. Status and privilege also
have a huge bearing on how one is perceived or how one imagines
one is seen. European perpetuated mythologies surrounding and
endorsing hierarchy, functioning alongside the management of fear
and the displays of arrogance, form part of the necessary conditions required to maintain colonial power. The 'wind of change',[2]
however, was unstoppable. By 1960 most of black Africa, following
Ghana's lead in 1957, had fought for and won independence.

Both the terms and conditions of independence and the theatre
of Cold War politics impacted hugely on the new states in Africa.
Europe and the United States were determined to influence the political direction of the new African independent states, and through
covert neo-colonial operations managed to hang onto and determine
the future political direction of many of these new countries. The
divide and rule policy utilised by the West was epitomised by the
brutal murder of Patrice Lumumba in 1961. Lumumba was the first
democratically elected prime minister of the Republic of the Congo
and a pioneer of African Unity.

It's not surprising, then, that when we look at this series of
photographs, we recognise traces of colonial subjugation and postcolonial trauma. These photographs connote the complex condition
of African modernity, framed somewhere between the past and the
future, between tradition and progress. The fact that old and the
new Africa can exist simultaneously is rarely recognised, a condition
that marks the continent as being on the one hand strangled by what
Fanon identified as:

A bourgeoisie similar to that developed in Europe [that] is able to elaborate an ideology and at the same time strengthen its own power. Such a bourgeoisie, dynamic, educated and secular, has fully succeeded in its undertaking of the accumulation of capital and has given the nation a minimum of prosperity ... This get-rich-quick middle class shows itself incapable of great ideas or inventiveness. It remembers what it has read in European textbooks and imperceptibly it becomes not even the replica of Europe, but its caricature.[3]

On the other hand, it is released through the recognition of an Afropolitan perspective of the self, aimed at a future that must unhinge the stereotype, which confidently claims that:

There is that deep abyss of Culture, ill-defined at best. One must decide what comprises 'African culture' beyond filial piety and pepper soup. The project can be utterly baffling –whether one lives in an African country or not. But the process is enriching, in that it expands one's basic perspective on nation and self-hood. If nothing else the Afropolitan knows that nothing is neatly black and white, that to be anything is to be sure of who you are uniquely.[4]

This is part of the tension that resides in *Hotel Afrique* – we know that under the lavish veneer there is a deeply troubled and complex body politic that cannot be covered up.

2007

NOTES

1 Binyavanga Wainaina, 'How to Write about Africa', *Granta*, 92, 2005.

2 From an address by Harold Macmillan to members of both Houses of the Parliament of the Union Of South Africa, Cape Town, 3 February 1960. Available at https://web-archives.univ-pau.fr/english/TD2doc1. pdf, accessed 10 January 2022.

3 Frantz Fanon, *The Wretched of The Earth*, Penguin: Harmondsworth, 1961, p141.

4 Taiye Selasim, 'Bye-Bye, Barbar' or 'What is an Afropolitan?', www. thelip.robertsharp.co.uk, 3 March 2005.

Black Atlantic

13

Ward Four and More

Mark Sealy: Why was photography so important for you?

Earlie Hundall: Well, I guess it evolved from my childhood, knowing that my grandmother and my father would make pictures of us on special holidays. My grandmother kept this photo album and when she would be sitting on the porch telling us about how things worked when she was a girl growing up, she would always refer to the photo album. At an early age I began to understand the importance of documenting one's community. I guess that was in the back of my mind the whole while. When I joined the Marine Corps, I purchased a small camera and began to document things around me, not knowing that I would become a photographer, or that would become the centre of my life.

MS: It's really the sense of grandma collecting the family album and local knowledge that inspired you?

EH: Right. She was very meticulous, she was the treasurer of her church circle and she read a lot. We lived next door to my grandmother. She was almost like the family historian. For me, that was important.

MS: It's interesting that it is the women in the house that are keeping all this knowledge safe.

EH: That is very true.

MS: So, then you joined the military and that's an important time, obviously. I know you spent critical time in Vietnam and experienced active service, but that must have also been really important in the formation of how you saw yourself in the world? This is the Cold War, and you're at the forefront of it. This is American imperialism overseas and racism at home. It must have been an incredibly complex time to be wearing an American uniform and then thinking about how we record our lives?

EH: I guess so, but I never really thought of it quite that way. I was working in Chicago at the steel mill, then I end up getting a letter from a good friend of mine telling me all about the Marine Corps. I left Chicago in December 1965, went home and decided to join the Corps in January 1966. I said if I had to go, I'd go with the best. A lot of guys were being drafted, so I joined the Corps.

After boot camp I thought back to the time of my father's photographs and I purchased a small camera, and began to just make pictures when it was possible. Even in Vietnam I made a few pictures. This is how my career as a photographer started. Composition and things came to me so natural. To me, it was like second nature, like I had been using a camera the whole while.

MS: You came home, which is a very important moment, especially to African-American servicemen. The incidence of racism went up because some didn't want the black soldiers to feel as though they had equal rights. I often think the guys that came home from Vietnam went as one thing, and then come home as something else. I don't know whether that's a fair comment …?

EH: It is, in a way. I came back to the States by ship. We came into Long Beach, California. The band was playing, the miniskirts were out at that time, it was a joyful kind of event. I took a plane and went back to Hattiesburg, Mississippi, and was home.

These were some of the changes that I incurred, but after that I was sitting around home. Then the Marine Corps recruiter came to my house one day, he was trying to talk me into going back into service, and I almost agreed, until my mother came out of the house and said 'no, no, no'. So that's how that ended.

MS: You left the army and you are heading off to art school, right? So you leave Mississippi …

EH: … On a Greyhound bus.

MS: You join art school, you study your program, and the camera was always with you?

EH: It was Juneteenth, 1969. I met a guy on campus named Nathaniel Sweets, his father was a newspaper editor. I told him, 'Hey man, I have a camera.' He said, 'Why don't you go and get it?' So I went into my room, I got my camera, we made some pictures. One day I had a problem and he said, 'You need to go see Mr Evans, the photography instructor.' I went to Mr Evans, knocked on the door, he came and said, 'Yes, sir?' I said, 'Mr Evans, I am having a problem, why am I getting spots on my negatives?' He took it and held it up to the light, looked at it and said, 'You're not agitating.' I said, 'Agitating?' He said, 'Yes, sir', and he closed the door.

MS: I love that.

EH: Another time I was walking down the hallway in the art department. Some of the kids had told me, 'Hudnall, there's a dark room here, you need to ask Dr Biggers'. I saw John Biggers walking down the hallway wearing a white dashiki, white pants and sandals with white socks on. I said, 'I heard there's a dark room in the art department and I was wondering if I can use it?' He said, 'Sure man,' reached his hand in his pocket and gave me the key. No instruction or anything.

MS: I love the idea that a professor at a university says to a young person, 'Here you go, here's the key.'

EH: All of this was instant, it wasn't planned. Like how I got into the Houston community. Dr Freeman at the university was with the Model Cities Program, which was a program for community residents to understand and to take advantages of the city services that were offered. I was painting a mural on the wall in Hannah Hall and Dr Freeman walked up to me and said, 'Are you Earlie Hudnall?' I said, 'Yes, I am'. He said, 'Mr Evans sent me to you. I need a photographer. Will you come to my office and talk to me?'

This is how I was thrust into the Fourth Ward area, an area that was founded by freed slaves. So I was able to go into that neighbourhood, and the closeness of the community was similar to what I had grown up around in Mississippi. The people were friendly, the kids were playing in the streets, people were sitting on their porches, talking to someone next to them on their porch. You can see the skyline of the city in the background and how that played upon the community, and the closeness of the working people moving about.

MS: You felt at home, being transported through this invitation to document this community, and that becomes the catalyst for you feeling, 'Hold on a minute, I know these people because I am these people.'

EH: Correct. Then wherever I would go, I wanted to get off the beaten path to find out how people live, what they did day to day. That became so important to me.

MS: Did you feel as though what you were doing was unique and quite important, or were you just intuitively making these people visible?

EH: I was intuitively making them visible because it was a joy. I guess socially I was somewhat of an introvert, but the camera allowed me to have a status, to move about, to enjoy.

MS: I think we really need to emphasise that people embraced your presence, knowing and trusting that you weren't going to be producing things that were going to replicate some awful stereotype around black communities in American society.

EH: That is so true.

MS: So, your photographic life becomes an intimate, entangled and joyous relationship with the people of the First, Second, Third and Fourth Ward, a sense that you are familiar with that space. They're also familiar with you, right?

EH: For me, it's difficult sometimes. It's like a projector: you back it up to the beginning and you start all over again. Throughout the day, my thoughts and my visual interpretation go all the way back, from early childhood to the time I was in military service and the time that I was in college. Events just pop up – boom – and it's the memories, you know, you have to deal with those.

Some things are tragic – I used to follow the fire truck, follow the ambulance – and a lot of things are very joyful – family events and things of this nature. That is a constant reminder and it reinforces, now more than ever, the importance of what I'm doing. This is my thrust: to continue doing what I've been doing for the last fifty years, to continue to document life.

MS: What's interesting is that it's almost as if you are a welcome guest in these spaces, from mothers hugging their children, little boys standing to attention when an uncle arrives – they are almost ignoring you.

EH: You have interpreted correctly. You know, I very seldom, almost never, asked a person permission to make a photograph verbally. Their permission comes through our way of greeting each other, out of respect for, and not interfering with, that individual. I think for me, when I approach my subjects, very cautiously, very carefully and respectfully, you know, the permission is granted to me.

MS: There is a sense of empathy and a sense of acknowledgement that you are in that space. It's like a community embrace, right?

EH: For me, it's very natural to pick up my camera, to drive into an area and to get out and to walk. When you walk within a community, you are at what you can consider Ground Zero, eye level. You actually see what's going on, you smell and visualise, you compose, all in an instant.

MS: This is a day in the life of Earlie, right? This is the everyday, this is a place of just being and recognising, not necessarily talking to the place all the time, but allowing it to be quietly visualised, collected and brought together. Our lives are often framed by others through a lens of some kind of violence. What's great about your work is that it feels like a neighbourhood. When people turn up in places that they're not familiar with, some of these neighbourhoods can look quite harsh. The reality is that these communities survive through care.

EH: That is so true. The neighbourhood is really a sanctuary to the community, and the neighbours understand and know how to more or less survive. I think that everybody wants the same things, the same comfort in life, but people in a community make their own personal adjustments.

MS: Finally, Earlie, what would you ideally want from the work?

EH: Personally, for me, nothing. For the viewer, I hope that whoever looks at it, whoever can identify with it, can carry something back that would enhance them, whether it's personal or it's something that causes them to react. But I hope that the reaction that people get from my work is all positive. This is all that I can ask from the viewer. For me, personally, after I have made the image, I feel that my work is done.

This interview originally appeared in Hapax Magazine, *No. 1, Autumn/Winter 2021/22.*

14

James VanDerZee:
Harlem's Black Photographer

In many respects, James VanDerZee, black America's greatest photographer, was fortunate in his origins. Born in Lenox,
Massachusetts, in 1886, he grew up in an environment that encouraged his artistic and intellectual development. His parents, John and
Susan VanDerZee, were economically independent, employed by
wealthy white families who owned houses around Lenox (for a time
they worked as maid and butler for Ulysses S. Grant). And although
bigotry and racial prejudice unquestionably existed in turn-of-the-
century New England, they do not seem to have played much part
in James's childhood.

He played both the violin and the piano and showed an early
interest in pictures. He was surrounded by photographs of his
extended family, and often supplied illustrations and other art works
for his school. He obtained his first camera at thirteen, after answering
a magazine advertisement promising one in return for selling twenty
packets of perfumed sachet powder. This camera failed to live up to
his expectations but, undeterred, he saved what little money he could
earn waiting at tables in a local boarding house during the holidays
and bought a better one from a mail order company.

Like many photographers, VanDerZee made his first studies of
what was around him. His family and friends were the main focus
of his work, which he was now financing by working as a waiter
full-time. (His father, being a respected career waiter, often provided
the references.) Then, in 1905, he followed his father to New York
and found work as a photographic assistant in a department store in
Newark, New Jersey. Before long he was more in demand than the
photographer he was working for.

He opened his first studio in Harlem in 1906 and soon developed a reputation among the residents as somebody who could produce sympathetic and flattering portraits. This was because he was consciously breaking the formal conventions and styles of the time. His pictures were informed by the romantic aesthetics of painting, and as his client base grew so did his confidence and his desire to experiment with backdrops and multiple exposures – techniques which both proved very popular.

One of his major objectives was to photograph black people in a positive light. Historically, photographic representations of black people have tended to focus on the black subject as aggressor, as exotic Other, or as victim of self-imposed tragedy. What makes VanDerZee's work so invigorating is the way it explodes the myth of a non-existent black middle-class in the early part of this century. As Val Wilmer has pointed out: 'VanDerZee had no part in recording squalor. Whether taking pictures at Madam Walker's salon or recording returning First World War veterans proudly displaying their medals, he was concerned with enhancing the quality of life for his subjects, not reminding them of injustice. His sitters came to have their portraits taken, and if life had put a few creases here and there, his retouching knife was there to smooth it away.'[1]

What is important about VanDerZee's photographs in Harlem is that they give us the opportunity to re-evaluate what it meant to be an African American in New York in the first half of the twentieth century. Even today, photographs of black Americans tend to present images of poverty and helplessness, of people locked into a dependency culture. VanDerZee, by contrast, focused on success and aspiration in black Harlem. But he did more than that. He produced a range of works which attempted to portray the emotions and sensibilities of his sitters, including some ethereal photographic montages that are a powerful testament to memory and loss. His 'mortuary portraits', produced in funeral parlours, are among the best examples of the way his photographs tackled difficult emotional terrain. VanDerZee's studio became a theatre in which the full range of black experiences were played out.

His work provides a unique insight into Harlem from a photographer who was not working towards a definitive, voyeuristic social statement. VanDerZee worked from the inside, relying on commissions from Harlem residents for his survival. He didn't merely photograph the 'Harlem Renaissance', the surge of artistic and intellectual creativity that began with the end of the First World War and ended with the Stock Market Crash of 1929, he was an important part of it.

In 1924, Marcus Garvey's United Negro Improvement Association commissioned VanDerZee to document many of its activities. Roger C. Birt, Associate Professor of Humanities at San Francisco State University, writes that 'Garvey wanted to blanket the black media with images of a vibrant and active UNIA under his own careful stewardship. He hired VanDerZee ... [who] proved himself to be as good a reporter as he was an imaginative artist.'[2] Both VanDerZee and Marcus Garvey were well aware of the politics of representation of the time.

Although the UNIA took him out on the streets, it was in his studio portraits that VanDerZee invested his greatest skills. According to the African-American historian, Deborah Willis-Braithwaite, his relatively comfortable background had given VanDerZee a strong, autonomous sense of self, which he was able to transfer on to his subjects, particularly when they entered the carefully constructed world of his studio.[3]

The high-street photographic studio is a special place in any community. It is a place where the subject comes to the camera rather than gets discovered by it. It is a place of equal exchange between sitter and photographer within a set environment. The sitter opens the dialogue; the photographer (especially VanDerZee, who had received training in the visual arts) responds by trying to produce a piece of work that his subject can both feel proud of and project his or her own fantasies on to. VanDerZee excelled in producing images in his studio that his constituency identified with, or wished to be recognised within. Most studio portraits are intended as a legacy, and he enabled his sitters to be remembered in the best possible light. His portraits show how a community wanted to be active in producing representations of themselves for themselves.

Much of his early success was due to the First World War. He took portraits of soldiers to give to their families and sweethearts, which were followed by commissions from families and sweethearts to send to their men. Like that of many other Harlem artists, his work blossomed during the 1920s, when he was the favourite portrait photographer of well-to-do Harlem residents, and even after the Depression took hold,

VanDerZee experienced little loss of custom. But during the 1940s, 1950s and early 1960s he turned increasingly to photo-restoration, which he had taught himself, in order to supplement his income.

By 1967, when he was discovered by Reginald McGhee, a young photographer researching the history of Harlem for an exhibition at the Metropolitan Museum of Art, VanDerZee and his second wife, Gaynella, were in serious straits. The exhibition, and the subsequent establishment of a VanDerZee Institute, provided them with a spasmodic but, in the end, adequate income. And as his work was discovered by new generations of African Americans, he enjoyed his own personal renaissance. Even in the later years of his life, black intellectuals, celebrities and the nouveau riche still commissioned him to take their portraits. His more celebrated clients included Jack Johnson, the first black world heavyweight boxing champion; Madame C. J. Walker, the first African-American woman to become a millionaire; Bill Cosby, the comedian, actor and producer; and the painter Jean-Michel Basquiat.

After Gaynella's death, VanDerZee married for a third time, in 1977, at the age of 91. He died in 1983. The tragedy is that recognition from the international photographic communities came to him so late in life – a situation which, according to Val Wilmer, is all too familiar: 'The fact remains that in the photography world, as elsewhere, the work of black photographers continues to be scandalously neglected in favour of exotic images and cultural caricatures produced by whites.'[4]

This text originally appeared in The Independent *in spring 1995.*

NOTES

1 Van Wilmer quoted in Rodger C Birt, 'VanDerZee Harlem Photographer', in *VanDerZee Photographer 1886-1983*, Deborah Willis-Braithwaite, Harry N Abrams, Inc., in association with The National Portrait Gallery, Smithsonian Institute, 1993, p48.

2 *Ibid.*

3 Deborah Willis-Braithwaite, 'They Knew Their Names', in *op. cit.*, Braithwaite, p10.

4 Birt, *op. cit.*, p48.

15

When Existence Alone
Is Constant Torture

Poverty is a trap that millions of people across the globe attempt to escape from on a daily basis. It causes extreme pain, mental stress and emotional heartbreak, both for those that leave their country of origin in search of work and for those that are left behind. What binds the departed or the 'burnt ones'[1] together is the drive to provide a dignified life for themselves and their families, and the faith that they too can secure a united future, if they have hope. When existence alone is constant torture, desperate acts of survival are performed, and as part of the journey – not to a new identity but to a life of no identity – death becomes a familiar final destination.

When existence alone is constant torture, the 'self extends out beyond the boundaries of the body, [and] occupies a space much larger than the body'.[2] In extreme circumstances, the extension of the self becomes a political referent that needs to be erased, hidden; a negated body to be exploited or, literally, exploded. A body extended, out of place, regarded as less than human and rendered nameless and, by extension, not real. The nameless who flee conflict, the refugee, the asylum seeker, the economic migrant and those held within regimes of violence, are all part of an extended mass of human life carelessly discarded.

People that Go No Go,[3] or those that dare to dream, take on the quest for freedom, understanding that they break with the convention of being cast as docile bodies for industrial consumption. They understand that the journey to freedom is not fluid; it stops at critical points, calculations and risks have to be assessed, and time becomes an asset and a burden. At borders, the hopeful ones cause chaos by refusing to disappear. They stay in focus by generating new hope in the idea of a promised land. (See Nikolaj Bendix Skyum Larsen's film *Promised Land* [2011]).[4] When bodies act, or call out, against extreme conditions of pain, they represent a threat and 'must be killed, since they seem to live on, stubbornly, in a state of deadness'.[5] It's at this juncture that the body becomes a symbolic marker of human failure and consumption.

The body's expanded space, through the critical situation of poverty and pain, has devastating effects on all those who see the body and refuse to act. In this moment, humiliation is not reflected in the face of the abject subject, but in the face of the passer-by or the audience. It's in our moment of passing, or our refusal to acknowledge human need, that the migrants, the refugees, the asylum seekers, the unemployed, the desperate and the mentally ill regain their humanity because when we walk by those in need, they become charged with a Medusa-like power that turns our gaze to stone. With each negation we become harder.

When the abject subject spills over into sanitised spaces, the idyllic Mediterranean beach, the airport, the art gallery, the shopping mall or media news channels it causes a rupture and generates resistance. These people become the spillage used for a neo-anthropological study that surfaces in the presence of a culture industry.[6] It's when unwanted tortured bodies become larger than the space of their bodies that we render them, and by extension humanity, invisible, which links to the notion of how and in what context a body on display becomes critically contested.

When existence is constant torture, the human body is vulnerable to being symbolically framed as pathetic. Viewing the pain of others from a position of privilege, pleasure or power does not guarantee empathy, but it does create the conditions for a regurgitated ideological merry-go-round of the image as spectacle, and for compassion fatigue.

At the crux of LaToya Ruby Frazier's photography is a critical and self-proclaiming response to the cultural baggage that has been dumped on her and her immediate family. Within the corpus of this work lies a sense of accusation that is aimed at the viewer; an accusation that highlights a disaffected but loving set of relationships that are, at times literally, laid bare for us to observe. The black body in Frazier's work becomes a resilient signifier that refuses to become invisible, even if America's corporate steel companies no longer require it.

The body, through her work, takes on new role. It performs the past in the present and laments that lost space where employment and aspiration have morphed into poverty and abandonment. Through the construction of the photograph, the image in focus is collapsed into the now. This is particularly evident in the portrait Ruby Frazier made with her mother titled *Momme* (2008). It forms part of a wider body of work titled *The Notion of Family* (2001-2014). Within this double portrait photograph, Ruby Frazier morphs the side profile of her mother with a frontal half self-portrait, producing a joined and abstracted image of mother and daughter, relaying to the viewer that they are both separate and uniform. Her mother's downcast eye is almost shut as if in resignation. In contrast, Ruby Frazier returns a hard, accusatory gaze back at the viewer as if to proclaim that the past lives on through her. As a photograph it functions beyond the mirror; it both obscures and reveals the physical, emotional and experiential relationship between them, ultimately allowing them to become one.

If the unwanted human body keeps on occupying spaces, refusing to be laid bare, and is brought into view, then the unwanted can't be coded out of society or transformed into mere historical numbers. This is the work Frazier's photographs do. History has taught us that when the human form is transformed into a number, the consequences are disastrous – we lose sight of our humanity and kill with ease. In this moment we lose focus, withdrawing from the reality of the situation and constructing utopias or fantasy politics based on a nation's glorious and imagined 'pure' past.

The bad old days of 'struggle to exist' become the good old days of today. The present is so horrific for many of the world's peoples as they increasingly become city dwellers, unofficially expanding the borders and boundaries of urban space. 'When its borders begin to be blurred, the bare life that dwelt there frees itself in the city and becomes both subject and object of the conflicts of the political order, the one place for both the organization of state power and emancipation from it.'⁷

This leads us to the inevitable questions of how one arrests the development of a condition in which the machinery of progress operates at an unstoppable and all-consuming pace. How much human life rendered as waste is acceptable? What is the role of the photographic image when considered a tool for salvaging a life long since lost? What part, then, do we collectively play in the demise of our own emancipation and of our own futures, either as victims or advocates for change, if we don't take action beyond a zone of reflection?

This text originally appeared in Next Level Magazine *in 2013 and was revised in 2021.*

NOTES

1 Yto Barrada, *A Life Full of Holes: The Strait Project*, Autograph ABP in association with Photoworks, The Mead Gallery and Witte de With Center for Contemporary Art, 2005, p57.

2 Giorgio Agamben, *Homo Sacer: Sovereign Power and Bare Life*, Stanford University Press: California, 1988, p33.

3 A.V. Denderen, *Go No Go*, Actes Sud: Arles, 2003.

4 *Promised Land* (2011), Nikolaj Bendix Skyum Larsen, 50 minutes, HD 3-screen projection, 5.1 surround sound. *Promised Land* portrays Mohammed, Jafar, Hasan, Camron, Khan, Reza and his three year old son, Nima – young migrants who will go to any length to cross the Channel from the French seaport town of Calais to enter Britain in the hope of finding a better life. The multiple screens in Nikolaj Bendix Skyum Larsen's *Promised Land* combine beautiful cinematography with footage captured by migrants, to give a deep insight into their close friendships: their hopes, dreams and ways of coping with the misery of their situation, their journeys from war-torn regimes, and dangerous attempts at getting into Britain – their Promised Land.

5 Judith Butler, *Precarious Life: The Power of Mourning and Violence*, Verso Books: London, 2004, p33.

6 M. Horkheimer and T. W. Adorno, *Dialectic of Enlightenment*, G. Schmitt-Noerr (ed), Stanford University Press: California, 2003.

7 Agamben, *op. cit.*, p12.

16

A Note from Outside

In late 1993 I was invited by the organisers of Africa 95 *to curate and co-coordinate a photographic programme. The aim was to complement an ambitious, nationwide season that would include all the visual arts, music, dance, cinema, literature, radio and television. The scheduled events were to take place during the last quarter of 1995.*

Partners for the visual arts programme included Tate Gallery in Liverpool with Vital: Three Contemporary African Artists; *The Barbican Art Centre exhibited* Technology, Tradition and Lurex: The Art of African Textiles; *The Whitechapel Art Gallery presented* Seven Stories About Modern Art in Africa; *and at the same time, The Birmingham Museum and Art Gallery produced a survey exhibition,* Siyawela: Love, Loss and Liberation in Art from South Africa.

Within the context of photography, I worked mainly with three nationwide galleries. At the Ikon Gallery in Birmingham, we presented an exhibition and publication titled Self Evident. *It included newly commissioned works by the UK-based artists Oladele Ajiboye Bamgboye, Ingrid Pollard and Maxine Walker. Their commission was to respond directly to the studio portraits by the Malian photographer Seydou Keita and the Senegalese photographer Mama Casset. The exhibition worked as a conversation concerning the studio as a performative space for identity formations.*

In partnership with The Photographers' Gallery in London, after spending some time in 1994 researching at the first Bamako Photography Festival, we agreed to focus on two young, contemporary African photographers: Samuel Fosso from Cameroon and the Guinean photographer, Mody Sory Diallo. The exhibition would show these promising young artists for the first time in the UK.

At the Impressions Gallery located in York, we staged a modest, one-person exhibition of Rotimi Fani-Kayode's colour works. I curated the show from Fani-Kayode's medium format colour photographs. He had produced these towards the end of his life while living with his partner Alex Hirst in a one-bedroom flat on Railton Road in Brixton. His colour works had received minimal exposure. The Africa 95 *season provided the perfect opportunity to bring Fani-Kayode's work national and international attention. Along with the exhibition, we produced a modest publication containing twelve colour photographs. I wrote the following essay for that book.*

Rotimi Fani-Kayode brought to his photographic work an attitude and an application that few institutions have been capable of understanding. On a superficial level, some of Kayode's early photographs of gay lifestyles were produced after a certain celebrated gay photographer, who has since been canonised around the world. Kayode was certainly aware of Mapplethorpe's work, yet his photographs were never derivative of Mapplethorpe's. However, this subject area has been rigidly defined by curators, and is repeated as and when the marketplace can sustain new offerings from the Mapplethorpe Estate. This laying down of rules, boundaries and borders by Eurocentric curators is how a canon is constructed.

Meanwhile, Kayode as an 'outsider' was given the burden of representing the Other. The unspoken rules are that as a black artist, you must make work that represents all of the 'race'. What Kayode was attempting to communicate was of little or no concern to the Eurocentric photographic trends of his time. What Kayode represented to the outside world would define the way his photographs would be read. This exhibition shows that Kayode was a photographer in his own right working within, and on, his own terms of reference, trying to establish his own presence within photography. This was done with the assistance of his partner, Alex Hirst. Together they produced a body of work that is a celebration of hybridity and cultural diversity across the boundaries of race and desire.

Kayode's main frustration was confrontation with egocentric institutional gatekeepers. When Kayode was trying to generate interest in his photographs he experienced, more often than not, that the gatekeepers were out to lunch and there was no reservation for him at the table. On the rare occasion when he/they could get an audience, curators found it difficult to grasp Kayode's terms of reference. Quite simply, his practice was not understood.

Kayode's agenda and the positions he adopted were often relegated to marginal interest groups. Ethnicity and sexuality, within mainstream gallery contexts, were dubbed 'too political'. Kayode's work was not seen as being in good taste or suitable for a gallery. Most works shown in these spaces addressed issues of sex and race while still subscribing to the classical traditions of Manet's *Olympia* or Gauguin's *Manao Tupapau*, or, if outside of this tradition, they were championed by an established art dealer. Kayode, along with many other black artists at this time, had no advocate or agent.

Kayode wanted to make interventions. His version of *Olympia*, *(White Bouquet)* (1987), was not a simple reversal of gender and race roles. This work was a direct attack on the institutional canons. *(White Bouquet)* is a challenge that says: 'I have done my homework; I have read your art history. This is what I want to do with that knowledge – invert, subvert and appropriate it – to suit my own concerns and experiences.'

Kayode's references in many of his photographs offer more than just a representation of the exotic or simply taking pictures for shock value. His photographs, as Wendy Grossman has pointed out, were not produced in a vacuum; they are informed studies.

> *White Flowers* [sic], in drawing upon a multiplicity of sources, displays the diversity of Fani-Kayode's work and background. In his use of montage and exploration of enigmatic visual occurrences, Fani-Kayode echoes the surrealistic style and illusive narrative of conceptual photographers such as Duane Michals and Jerry Uelsmann. Reflected in this image is the photographer's search for his own voice which led him through the fine and graphic arts to photography.[1]

Few galleries had time for a photographer concerned with his own 'African-ness'. Few magazines were interested in work produced by indigenous African photographers and if photographic works by African photographers were published, the tone was, and generally still is, patronising. Books and journals are still dominated by US and European photographers producing so-called 'definitive stories' for the Sunday supplements from some 'exotic' African location which, when published, often reproduce a stereotypical, racialised view that falls in line with the long history of misrepresentation of African cultures. It is only recently with the formation of organisations like *Revue Noire* and Autograph that progress has been made in redressing this situation by exhibiting, publishing and advocating work from Africa and the diaspora that shows there is a vibrant, complex photographic movement within the continent of Africa.

On occasions when curators and critics would attempt to decode Kayode's photographs, they would fall into producing lazy and crude comparisons with Mapplethorpe's work. The assumption has always been that Kayode wanted the mantle of Mapplethorpe – this was never the case. These and similar attitudes to Kayode's photographs led Kayode to write, 'Working in a Western context, the African artist inevitably encounters racism.'[2] Kayode was becoming more and more aware of the subtle forms of postcolonial racism that are endemic to Eurocentric institutions.

Within the UK, little work was being done with and about black photographers and artists in general, although there was a growing sense of agitation at the grassroots level. This was being animated by artists such as Eddie Chambers and Sunil Gupta, to name but a few (the issue was highlighted in the joint essay by Professor Stuart Hall and David A. Bailey for *Ten.8* magazine's *Critical Decade: Black British Photography in the 80s*, Vol. 2, Issue 3, entitled 'The Vertigo of Displacement'). Institutions appeared to have little interest or inclination to research and develop an understanding of practitioners like Kayode and their terms of reference. If black photographers/artists were to gain any ground then supportive collaborations and relationships had to be formed. Alex Hirst, Kayode's friend and lover, became one such collaborator, along with several other artists who were experiencing similar problems. Networks and lobby groups began to formulate ways of gaining visibility. Kayode was a key player within this formulation and indeed was the second chair of Autograph, when it was the Association of Black Photographers.

The series of works presented in this exhibition were produced towards the latter part of Kayode's life and were a celebration of his growing relationship with Alex Hirst. They show intriguing photographic scenarios that investigate issues relating specifically to race, sexuality and, most importantly, pleasure and desire. All the photographs are created within the studio context using models – Kayode did not subscribe to the notion of a decisive moment.

Each photograph represents a short narrative. Kayode's use of mise-en-scène, chiaroscuro and saturated, Rubenesque-like colours gives the works a tragic and theatrical quality, but at the same time offers us a sense of calm enhanced by the averted gaze of many of the models. This technique allows the viewer to feel comfortable within the act of looking; not being presented with direct eye contact seduces us into sustaining our gaze. The dramas in Kayode's work could either be past or present as the work does not locate or signify a specific time or place. This is the land of fantasy and desire, where date, time and location are irrelevant. The photographs generally represent an act. They are fragments of plays that Kayode and Hirst constructed which relate to dislocation and disruption. The recurring presence of masks is essential within this series of photographs, suggesting to the viewer that the surface is there to be challenged, but at the same time offering the subject a protective barrier.

The ethereal world was as important to Kayode as the tangible world. In his work, he is inviting us to play with him in the grey zones between black and white, gay and straight, acceptance and taboo. This work was the beginning of a constructed, twilight, cross-cultural zone, a kind of Neverland where 'reality' is a stranger. Within his later work, Kayode employed what Yoruba priests and artists call the 'technique of ecstasy', where concepts of reality are distorted or disrupted to produce ambiguous meanings. 'While these remain veiled for the uninitiated non Yoruba audience, when decoded they contribute to the unravelling of the multi-layered symbolism behind his work,' states Wendy Grossman.[3]

It was a fact that few people at that time had the capacity to unravel Kayode's work. That did, and still does, make it difficult for curators to make a reading of his photographs. He was often subjected to liberal ignorance and its patronising attitude towards his photographs and his cultural traditions. This situation is still experienced by many artists of colour today.

Kayode came from 'over there', dark, distant Africa; Nigeria. He wasn't supposed to be a photographer in Africa either, due to his family's social position. He wasn't supposed to expect Western galleries to take his work seriously. His confidence came from being born to the Balogun chief of Ife. His family were deeply rooted in Yoruba culture. The Kayode family were the keepers of the Shrine of Yoruba deities and priests of Ife. Kayode understood his cultural heritage. He did not have an 'identity crisis'. He knew exactly who he was and what he represented and how his lifestyle and work would impact those around him.

On three counts I am an outsider: in terms of sexuality; in terms of geographical and cultural dislocation; and in the sense of not having become the sort of respectably married professional my parents might have hoped for.

He was aware of the systems he was trying to penetrate. He wrote,

Europeans faced with the dogged survival of alien cultures and as mercantile as they were in the days of the Trade, are now trying to sell our culture as a consumer product. I am inevitably caught up in this.[4]

Kayode was at the forefront of blowing apart the stereotype. He resisted categorisation and labelling. He spent most of his life in the West. He was not an afro-essentialist. He was an African man with a camera who took the time and trouble to develop his technique. Kayode was no young pretender. Kayode understood photography both in technical terms and historically. He did not expect some fast track to success. He wanted his work to have an impact and at the same time educate both in the West and within the 'Third World':

Both aesthetically and ethically, I seek to translate my rage and my desire into new images which will undermine conventional perceptions and which may reveal hidden worlds. Many of the images are seen as sexually explicit – or more precisely, homosexually explicit. I make my pictures homosexual on purpose. Black men from the Third World have not previously revealed either to their own peoples or to the West a certain shocking fact: they can desire each other.[5]

1995

NOTES

1 Wendy Grossman, *Tradition & Transformation in African Photography: From Yoruba Ritual to Rotimi Fani-Kayode*, College Park: Maryland, 1993 (MA Thesis), p9. Grossman is referring to Fani-Kayode's work also known as *(White Bouquet)*.

2 Rotimi Fani-Kayode, 'Traces of Ecstasy', in David A. Bailey, Stuart Hall, Andy Cameron and Derek Bishton (eds), 'Critical Decade: Black British Photography in the 80s', *Ten.8*, Vol. 2, No. 3, 1992, p68.

3 Grossman, *op. cit.*

4 Fani-Kayode, *op.cit.*, p69.

5 *Ibid.*, p68.

17

A Gathering of Souls

Photographs brought together from different spaces, mindsets and cultures function as provocations dropped into the calm waters of our thoughts. They challenge our thinking, sometimes hiding the meanings buried within them, but clearly working as part of our process of trying to make sense of this world. For historically marginalised people, photographs, when presented with care, can help locate our missing chapters. Images keep people in life; when curated with dignity, they can resurrect cultures that have been denied visibility or made silent. They help us understand by holding up the making of our lives; they pause us, offering respite from the velocity of our existence. Photographs tease us with questions like, 'Was I there?' or 'Is that us?', 'Is it real?', 'Did I witness this event or simply imagine it?' Though photographs never provide the complete answers, they might, at times, adjust or reset our sense of reality. Most importantly, they can help us frame new questions, uncouple and delink us from harmful dominant narratives, and allow us to feel the presence of a past moment in the now of our time.

In some of the photographs in this book – drawn from the Wedge Collection, owned and curated by Kenneth Montague – the quest for freedom and personal liberty is made exquisitely evident. Many of the collection's photographs work to revitalise a sense of joy in resistance. We sense this in a black-and-white photo made by the Greenville, Mississippi–based studio photographer, Henry Clay Anderson, titled *Motorcycle Riders* (ca. 1960). The young African American couple oozes with pride and pleasure. Wearing the signs of rebellious youth – leather jackets and fashionable headgear – while sitting astride their powerful Harley Davidson Hydra-Glide motorcycle, the couple disrupts the stereotypical representations of African

American life in 1960s Mississippi. The image is a powerful motivator for a generation of young people on the move.

As a time-trapping process, photography continuously offers us the opportunity to reflect on the way we were and make real, in the present, what we have become. It also helps us to see beyond the limits of our own experience and into new horizons, so that we can dare to imagine what we might be in the future. When photographs are produced and cared for with a community at heart, they provide a stage for their makers, subjects and stakeholders to proclaim, 'This is me, we, and therefore us.'

Collecting such images together is also a form of care. The work a photograph does in culture is always complex; an image has no one decisive meaning. It shifts in time and bends to the present understanding of mind and place. When we look through the collection of photographs that Montague has built, we register both his care in bringing them together and the new meanings created in their gathering. These are pictures Montague deeply identified with and felt were missing from the official narrative, pictures he needed to see. He hews closely to his father's mantra, 'lifting as we rise', in his collecting, elevating the experiences of black lives, the artists who capture them and, in turn, viewers who identify with them. As a result of this dynamic, Montague's collection of photographs – made through the lens of the African and African diasporic experience – is a rare, insightful, radical and bold act of deliverance. The arc of Montague's collection allows for a mosaic set of adventures to congregate and claim the right for a people to inscribe meaning to their own lives.

A photograph taken by the Jamaica-born, Birmingham-based British photographer Vanley Burke, *Boy with Flag* (1970), immediately opens a portal back to my childhood. Like Winford Fagan – the subject of this photograph – I, too, was busy building makeshift bicycles, enjoying the freedom cycling offered. If, like Fagan, you managed to fit a pair of cow-horn handlebars to your road-eating machine, it was infinitely wider, cooler and, therefore, more desirable. In the photograph, Fagan stands with his right hand confidently resting on his hip, willingly presenting himself to Burke's caring camera. He is relaxed as his presence in the park is recorded – and not by a stranger. Burke, we learned later, was known to Fagan and his family, and to the wider Handsworth community, for his photography. It's in this obvious moment of warmth between Fagan and Burke that we can begin to unpack the undercurrents at work in this seemingly peaceful moment.

Growing up in Handsworth, Birmingham in the 1960s and 1970s was, for black people, never simply about having a quiet ride in the park. In 2015, the *Guardian* interviewed Fagan as part of a series entitled *That's Me in the Picture*. In it, Fagan recalled that at the time of this photograph, 'there was a lot of racial hatred and gang violence. I remember being chased by skinheads, most of them a lot older than me, but some my age ... At the weekend we had more time to ourselves, and you'd run into gangs who went out to attack black people.' The Union Jack that Fagan attached to his bicycle was culturally and politically charged. As he informs us in that same interview: 'A union jack was something you would have then, not just for bunting. People asked me, "Why not a Jamaican flag?" but I didn't know about Jamaica. I was born here. My parents came here 50 or 60 years ago; I was one of the first generations.' With a greater understanding of Fagan's childhood and the social politics at work outside the frame of this photograph, we can begin to understand that his presence as a black subject in a public park flying a Union Jack marks him as being at risk, a child exposed daily to threats of racial violence. His bicycle, in the time and space of this photo-graph, becomes more than just an object of pleasure; it functions as a potential means of escape from those that despise his presence in Britain and his flying of the Union Flag. The photograph is powerful in that, for a brief moment, the atmosphere of hate that invisibly engulfs both Fagan and Bruke becomes insignificant.

Images assist us in understanding multiple narratives of history. *Boy with Flag* celebrates, locates, and anchors the young black British subject in history, and its radicality as an image provides us with the opportunity to see what it means to embrace and protect those who are most vulnerable in our society. The photograph also opens a portal to discussions of British imperialism's global impact and the ongoing violence this entangled legacy entails. It's forceful, playing simultaneously to the joy and pain of Fagan and Burke's shared condition.

A community can only survive when care is present, and Burke's work confirms the vital role that photography plays in the act of people caring for each other. Burke has not taken anything away from Fagan – the experience of his childhood remains intact – yet he has given his likeness new meaning in the archives of photography. Burke's camera in the park on that day in 1970 went beyond photography and memory. What Burke gave Fagan was a gift that would transcend space, time, politics and photographs. It was the gift of self-esteem that resonated, slowly but surely, through Handsworth's black community and beyond. Many years later, Fagan's wife would use Burke's photograph as the image on an invitation to her husband's fortieth birthday party.

Photographs are vehicles that transport us both to known and unknown places in our minds. They hold our multiple identities, and are essential keys to our cognitive world. They function as visas for our future journeys because what we see in the past helps formulate our future. Photographs open sensory space. I have never forgotten the moment when I watched a black mother stroke a photographic image of her deceased child while calling out his name. It was one of the few moments when photography broke me down not because of what I had seen, but because of the deep well of meaning that event extracted from me. Photographs help us connect to our lived experience's emotional terrain; they direct us to our core baselines.

Montague's photographic collection underlines the fact that black identities are unfixable and that photography, when used as a tool for making the internal human condition visible, becomes a source of infinite possibilities regarding constructions of the self and those we identify with through real or imagined codes, signs or languages. It's here that the magic of desire, different cultures and emotional states can be brought into visibility, laid bare, demystified or recoded.

Carrie Mae Weems taught us something extraordinary when she produced her exquisite work *The Kitchen Table Series* (1990), in which the kitchen table's domestic space is centre stage. Here, the rollercoaster of life's emotional states is served up for inquiry. Weems, through her autobiographical camera, invites us strangers to sit at her table of life; we are welcome but silent guests, unable to offer comfort, share the joy or act in the scene. As viewers, we become voyeurs. As guests, we can only observe as the girl inherits the older woman's relationship to her own reflected image. Here we can feel, by our proximity to Weems' subjects, the invisible transference of shared culture. In this tabled episode, the two protagonists have become one, bound by what 'making up to face the world' represents. As we observe the older woman and the young girl preparing themselves in their respective mirrors, we as an audience are invited to witness a form of cross-generational gender formation performed in the most everyday domestic scenario. The mirrors on the kitchen table signify distinctive gateways to the outside world. Even though the protagonists are divided by age (time) and experience (knowledge), they both seem to understand that in the act of sharing the space of self-preparation, there is no escape from the domains of representation at work in their lives. In framing this scenario for an audience, Weems has invited us to think through the conventions of the everyday moments that make up who we are, and how representation works on us.

When brought together in a considered, congregational way, photographs can function as a magic hall of mirrors; some of their reflections appear unfamiliar, dislocating and strange, while others seem brilliantly clear, honest, humorous distortions or close friends. If each time we visit the mirror we have changed, then the same applies to a photograph's effect on us. The unfairness of a photograph is that it stays still while we have no choice but to move on. It's in this hall of mirrors that a photograph does its best work on time and space – fuelling memories, igniting the imagination and opening up our multidimensional selves.

Photographs grip us, frighten us and taunt us. They encourage us to turn away and not see what is often most evident and cruel in humanity. Critically though, the essential aspect of a photograph is that it helps us share and celebrate our myriad ways of becoming. When they are gathered together with a sense of heart in mind, what emerges is a fuller language for understanding how the making of our collective soul is seen. African and African diasporic photographers have played an incredible role in framing the understanding of who we are. Joy Gregory, Liz Johnson Artur, Seydou Keïta, Deana Lawson, Zanele Muholi, Eustaquio Neves, and James Van Der Zee, among many, many others, all form part of a community of trans-African dream catchers whose images collectively and consciously work against the slow tide of negative representations that have historically engulfed the black body.

The collection of photographs gathered here signpost a different direction of travel for the black subject. This collection places the black subject front, back and centre stage in photography – as producers and as equal subjects of inquiry. Here, the black body is not a distant bag carrier, an emaciated victim or a broken, war-torn figure rendered only as a dead history. Here, the black subject is a living, inspiring, loving and aspirational subject, innovative and full of knowledge, transforming and claiming their rightful place in time. The Wedge Collection points to a place of pleasure and challenges the old discourses surrounding photography's history. Montague's gathering provides an opportunity to build new knowledge and join the dots differently, to assist in establishing a new conceptual map of the world. He has formulated a dynamic photographic treasure trove where the image of the black subject is allowed to shine, untroubled and protected from the old imperial pirates.

This essay was originally produced for As We Rise: Photography from the Black Atlantic: *Selections from the Wedge Collection* (*Aperture 2021*).

18

On Faisal Abdu'Allah

I first encountered *I wanna kill Sam 'cos he ain't my mother-fucking uncle*, Faisal Adbu'Allah's steel portraits, in November 1993 as part of an exhibition at the Photographers' Gallery in London entitled *Presences*. The five pieces on show were two-metre tall, one-metre wide, silkscreen, black ink prints on mild steel. They showed a series of young black men who looked as if they had just emerged from a Los Angeles rap music video and had etched themselves onto the gallery wall.

On encountering these images, I remember thinking that this was a very brazen body of work, full of cheek and boldness, but refreshing at the same time because it exuded confidence. This was reinforced by the cold, precise production values incorporated within the work.

One of the portraits in particular interested me, *Raham*. Out of the cold steel comes the image of a black man dressed in baggy jeans, hooded sweatshirt (with the hood up), denim jacket, big, military style boots and a shoulder bag. He is standing in a sideways position with his arm raised, pointing a silver handgun directly out of the frame at the audience. His eyes are focused straight down the barrel of the gun, where he fixes the viewer in his sights. The drama is intensified by the ring on his finger, which is in the form of the Muslim star and half-moon. The identification with Islam in *Raham* intensifies the drama.

In *Raham*, Faisal Abdu'Allah has constructed many of the anxieties and tensions that have historically surrounded images of black men. *Raham*, the image, is not 'safe'. He is black, armed and must therefore be dangerous, deemed to be a threat. The whites of his eyes are all we are presented with. We are denied access to any of the other facial attributes of Raham. The fist and gun are his face and in yours. This is a very 'hard' image.

However, the process of printing the works onto steel softens the initial impact of the work. The black and steel grey tones are not sharp. They fragment the image, giving the effect that the figure is emerging or disappearing into a heavy, cold fog. Raham is appearing before you in the guise of a grey haze, an urban nightmare and a steely vision. Is he ghostly or ghastly?

The confrontations set up in the work are therefore not purely about the potential for physical violence; the issue of psychological damage is also being investigated by Abdu'Allah. For a brief moment, Abdu'Allah gives the audience the opportunity to allow themselves to be threatened. *Raham* acts, then, as a catalyst for the viewer to get a sense of what it feels like to be under threat, a psychological, if not actual, state familiar to many young black men. *Raham* represents a displacement of the sense of threat. The work is a staged manifestation of those anxieties. It is an investigation into the act of 're-memory'. The work begs the question, who is frightened of whom?

The uncluttered surroundings force us to pay attention to the detail of Raham's clothes and accessories. *Raham* is as much about style as it is about violence – it becomes representative of an ideal. Faisal Abdu'Allah, by taking Raham out of an urban setting, has attempted to construct him as a symbol (the work is very referential of a fashion shoot).

What *Raham* symbolises is, of course, not fixed. To those who identify with the rap scene, *Raham* is archetypal, delivering many of the now expected clichés that the image of rap has come to represent. To those who have an investment in politically correct images of black men, *Raham* would probably be read as failing to offer 'dem black youth' a good role model. To those who fear black people, *Raham* is a worst-case scenario. The potency of Abdu'Allah's work is built on this dilemma. What is correct?

The success of this image is in fact that it is a manifestation of all that which is supposed to be negative about black young men. After all, what could be more threatening than having a gun pointed directly at your head? However if we look past the gun we see Raham is isolated, contained and alone, fixed in the cold steel. Is he asking us to back off, to leave him alone? After all, his has a history that means he has had to adopt the defensive position physically, psychologically, socially and culturally. Is it possible Raham could be seen as a defender of something good?

The pursuit of knowledge is a key concern for Abdu'Allah. In an interview I conducted with him for the Chiltern Sculpture Trust, he said: 'The work questions perceptions of race, culture and history, it puts the viewer in contact with both physical and mental aggression, the latter forced on us by the media.'[1]

Raham can be seen as a contestation aimed at agitating the notion that representation is a burden. Faisal Abdu'Allah is confident with what he and his work represent – he is very much a product of the 1990s. Abdu'Allah doesn't come from the generation that 'keeps an eye on the prize'. He is quite happy to stare directly at the 'prize', place both hands on it and carry it off.

The strength of Abdu'Allah lies in the fact that he has an uncanny knack of placing burdens back on his audience: you either subscribe or you don't. Faisal Abdu'Allah's works are not only about reflection, they're intrinsically about absorption and excavation.

1999

NOTE

1 From an interview with the artist commissioned by the Chiltern Sculpture Trust. The interview was published in 1999 as a forty-page booklet, illustrated in black and white by Faisal Abdu'Allah, called *Reservoir of Gods*.

Aïda Muluneh (*Memory of Hope* series; *The Mirage of Hope*, 2017). Photograph © Aïda Muluneh. Used with permission.

Aïda Muluneh (*Memory of Hope* series; *The American Dream*, 2017). Photograph © Aïda Muluneh. Used with permission.

Wilfred Ukpong, *Are My Dreams Too Bold For The Carbon Skin I Bear #1?* Courtesy of Wilfred Ukpong and Blazing Century Studios, Nigeria.

Wilfred Ukpong, *Forever We Are Bound To This Land By Blood #1.* Courtesy of Wilfred Ukpong and Blazing Century Studios, Nigeria.

Wilfred Ukpong, *By and By, I Will Carry This Burden Of Hope, Till The Laments Of My Child Is Heard #2*. Courtesy of Wilfred Ukpong and Blazing Century Studios, Nigeria.

Wilfred Ukpong, *Strong, We Believe In The Power Of This Motile Thing That Will Take Us There #2*. Courtesy of Wilfred Ukpong and Blazing Century Studios, Nigeria.

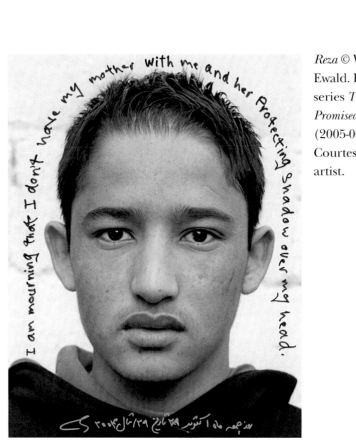

I am mourning that I don't have my mother with me and her protecting shadow over my head.

Reza © Wendy Ewald. From the series *Towards A Promised Land*, (2005-06). Courtesy the artist.

Installation view of *Reza* on the seafront at Margate. © Wendy Ewald.

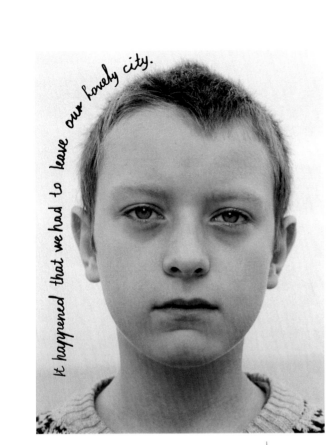

Uryi © Wendy Ewald. From the series *Towards A Promised Land* (2005-06). Courtesy the artist.

Installation view of *Uryi* on Dreamland Buildings in Margate. © Wendy Ewald.

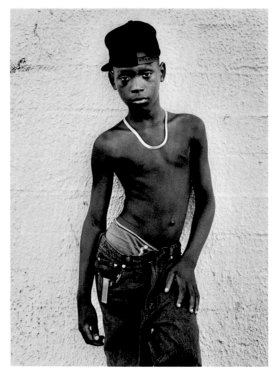

Earlie Hudnall, Jr., *Hip Hop*, 1993, gelatin silver print. Photograph © Earlie Hudnall, Jr.

Earlie Hudnall, Jr., *Lady With Flag*, 1994, gelatin silver print. Photograph © Earlie Hudnall, Jr.

Earlie Hudnall, Jr., *Street Ball*, 1993 gelatin silver print.
Photograph © Earlie Hudnall, Jr.

Earlie Hudnall, Jr., *Girls Run The World*, 2018 gelatin silver print. Photograph © Earlie Hudnall, Jr.

Earlie Hudnall, Jr., *Baldwin Flying Hands*, 1993 gelatin silver print. Photograph © Earlie Hudnall, Jr.

Khan, photographed at
Master's Art Studio, 1982.

Raja Salim, circa 1964-65.

Gordonbhai Bhakta at
Masterji's home studio,
Widdrington Road,
1957-68.

Mr and Mrs Khan, circa 1967.

Photographs from the series *From Here to Eternity* (1999).
Photographs © Sunil Gupta. Courtesy the artist.

Chicago

Hoist

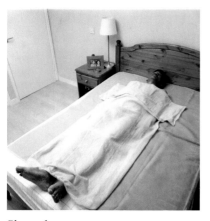

Shroud

Pleasuredrome

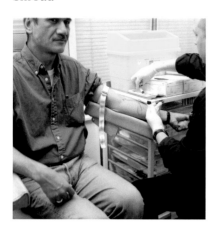

Blood

Fort

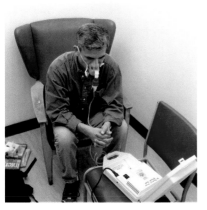

Pentamadine

Attitude

Christmas

Substation

Babe

Fist

Photographs from the series *Illustration of Life* (2003).
Photographs © Max Kandhola. Courtesy the artist.

Still, Room with Sunlight

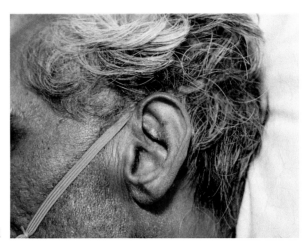

Ear 1

Blood
Transfusion 1

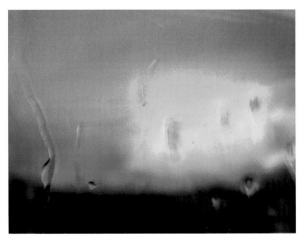

Urine Movement
in Bag 1

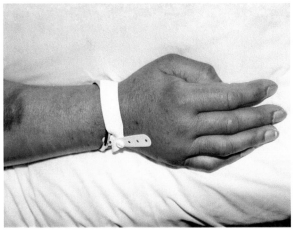

Name Tag and
Kara

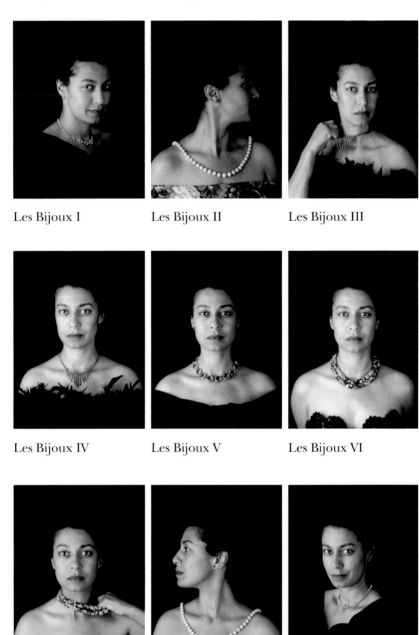

Les Bijoux I   Les Bijoux II   Les Bijoux III

Les Bijoux IV   Les Bijoux V   Les Bijoux VI

Les Bijoux VII   Les Bijoux VIII   Les Bijoux IX

Future-Facing People

19

Critical Conjunctures

High-profile black artists and curators, such as Keith Piper and David A. Bailey, owe some of their success to a cluster of publicly funded organisations – Autograph and iniva to name but two – that have not only nurtured ethnically diverse art but lobbied funders and established galleries for a fair deal. Mark Sealy asks Professor Stuart Hall to map out the major developments of the past decade or so, and to comment on the challenges facing these organisations in the post-Thatcher era.

Mark Sealy: In the 1980s there was much talk about the burden of representation (about what is produced by and for whom and who's allowed to speak on behalf of whom). Now we have a generation of individualistic, post-Thatcherite photographers who are reluctant to take on all that baggage. I wonder if they see organisations like Autograph[1] as still being representative?

Stuart Hall: I think these are big and very tricky questions and you have to have a rough history in mind. You have to think about the 1970s, in which there was no visibility, and the organising around that. What was being emphasised was that people were speaking from 'the black experience', the experience of displacement, the burden of race, etc. Quite early on, almost anybody of quality became ambiguous and critical about being unambiguously read as speaking for 'the race'. There was no doubt that that was how it was seen from the outside; people would say, he's a black photographer. And by saying that they would expect a certain kind of subject matter, a certain kind of exploration, a certain kind of politics and so on. The 1980s was already a break up of that because people were no longer refusing to acknowledge that they came from a particular tradition and political context, but they were insisting on the complexity and multiplicity of that. So there were many black experiences. There were a variety of migrant experiences and many Asian traditions. Anyhow, this was happening within a displaced diaspora in the West. People were no longer relating to a single identity, a single place of origin. They were not speaking unambiguously on behalf of that. They were very concerned about being driven back into an ethnic ghetto. Then, into the 1990s, that trend has gone even further. Nowadays people don't want to have the racial or ethnic signature attached to their work in any decisive way. They want to be seen as individual artists saying something distinctive. This is not as simple as it seems because they don't want to be plugged into the general British or European market – sink or swim. They want a little bit of the protectiveness which is gained by being part of a collective consciousness or a distinctive historical experience. But they don't want to be policed by it, they don't have to refer to it. One of the ways this manifests itself is in a much greater aesthetic confidence and sophistication. If it doesn't work aesthetically, they don't want it to work because it's black. They want it to work because it works. This is a kind of insistence on the formal quality of the work and discussion about its quality in aesthetic terms. This is very important because before now – and we can't disguise this – relatively poor work could get away with giving the right political message or coming from the right place. You might almost say this is what is involved in the movement from an identification as Afro-Caribbean, say, to being black British. In that move there is both a loss and a reaching for another kind of space from which to speak.

I think your question is: how do we assess this? The joker in the pack is what you said, Thatcherism, because there is no question that these are also the black children of Thatcherism. One of the things Thatcherism did was to open up interstices in society, not through the organised collective politics of equal opportunities, knocking on the door of the Arts Council and requiring collective representational space, but more a kind of hustling. To tell you the truth, there are no better hustlers around than our folks! So I don't think we can deny the fact that while refusing to centre the black experience in their work, these artists, nevertheless, are much more individualistically minded, they don't want to be represented as a group. They want the advice and the support that, say, Autograph can give them and they want to get into the mainstream. You might say this is only a minority, and it's quite true. But I think that hustling is the temper of the times. It represents a loss of some things and a set of gains. *These are not kids apologising for who they are.*

MS: The 1990s has witnessed the rise of the arts organisation – partly because bureaucracies are better than individual artists at competing in a new climate of mixed funding. Autograph and iniva[2] are just two which are acting on behalf of ethnically diverse artists as 'institutional advocates'. They are making it easier than ever to fund a good idea.

SH: Since the publication of *Ten.8*'s 'Critical Decade' issue[3] in 1992, the impetus has moved to a kind of organisational base in photography and the visual arts more generally. It means there can be a more consistent policy toward getting people exhibited, to giving the kind of initial support to young visual artists that they need just to get things visible at all. It's a big shift. I think we imagined that the end of the 1980s was the end of public funding and that everybody would have to go into the marketplace and that the marketplace would not be interested in culturally diverse work. Actually, people like Autograph have adapted to a mixed mode and moved out into the world of commercial photography, and so on, while maintaining a particular attention to the audiences they were created to nurture ...

MS: Autograph and iniva nurture and commission work which is exhibited in partnership with mainstream cultural institutions. In the 1980s these spaces were reluctant to enter into long-term collaborations with such organisations. Is this still the case?

SH: iniva, for example, is known about. Its individual way of working is recognised, but they are still fighting to be accepted as a legitimate partner by the mainstream. They still see iniva as something they will deal with once or twice when they have a particular kind of show they are interested in. It's not impossible any longer to make an impact once or twice. It is more difficult to have a continuously rolling developmental programme in which you hold, on the one hand, a very independent set of practitioners who are willing to play ball (but don't want to be part of your stable for ever), and at the same time, negotiate the field of mainstream criticism which is, in many ways, untouched by the whole debate about cultural diversity. Really! When one thinks about some of the ways iniva's shows have been critically dealt with, you would think nothing has changed since the 1970s. There's a lot of slippage back to a much older way of boxing these institutions in.

MS: Where is the future of organisations like Autograph? I wonder if we should continue in the advocacy role ... or whether we can make a transition into, say, competing with art dealers, drawing from the stable of talent we are associated with.

SH: I don't think the organisations have much choice. They've got to go in that direction. The question is if it's possible, both institutionally and creatively, to combine a continuing function of advocacy in relation to young practitioners who – without the experience of people like you – might give up. I feel that that level of support is still required, but that it cannot be enough any longer and that the scene has moved on so much that it is requisite for us to identify a well-established body of independent practitioners, who – largely through the organisations – are recognised as struggling for access to the mainstream outlets, whether they are private collectors or mainstream magazines or exhibition spaces, or whatever. Without it we will be seen as social work organisations in the arts, but not as able to compete in creative and aesthetic terms with the best that is going. Which is to say that we won't be seen as being at the forefront of what is going on – namely, *the cultural diversification of the mainstream itself.* That does imply that very serious, very experienced artists are continuously called on to represent what is most interesting in British mainstream art. So for that we need organisations with some experience and clout, with a history of successful advocacy and institutional staying power, but we also need them to move into some of these new spaces and to compete with them.

MS: We have just talked a lot about how things have changed for culturally diverse art in Britain, yet there is no consensus. In a recent essay in *Art Monthly*, Eddie Chambers used the comparison between the number of black people in service industries in the art world, and in the curatorial profession, to argue that very little has changed.

SH: I feel a lot has changed, too. I don't want to take an easy 'let a thousand flowers bloom' sort of position, but when you think of any cultural moment it always includes people who have different trajectories through it ... so you put a funny kind of frame over those varying generations, those different backgrounds. We have been so dependent on the creative flair and sustainability of a mere handful of people. There wouldn't be a scene without their work. I think that the most fruitful thing is to maintain an open space in which those different visions contend with each other. So, Eddie is going to want to go on insisting – as he always does – that there is an institutional racism which persists. You need that voice, though it may not necessarily appeal to your newcomer who is nineteen or twenty and wants to make images for the net. The dialogue between them will frame different collective practices. We have to think of career paths. If you just think of the number of exhibitions David A. Bailey has had a hand in (*Rhapsodies in Black* being just one), the people who have been shown through his curatorial endeavours, it is just a continual career. Sunil Gupta is another person who is institutionally enormously creative and inventive and whose personal work has changed a lot ... So these people change within themselves, the practices become new but they hold pivotal positions in different spaces. We couldn't have dreamed up the variety of people and careers which would have enabled this whole thing to survive. I like the plurality of it. I'm worried sometimes that the dialogue has broken down. I think of Eddie Chambers as somebody who is in conversation with these new developments in a way he wasn't five years ago and I think this is a welcome return after a period of abstention ... I am prepared to go with the diversity of styles and personalities. I don't think they are predictable but thank God they do arise, for where would we be without them?

This interview is edited from a conversation that first appeared in Creative Camera *in 1997 and later in* Creative Camera: 30 years of writing *(2000), edited by David Brittain.*

NOTES

1 Autograph ABP, a client of the Arts Council of England, was founded 1988 to promote work of African, Afro-Caribbean and Asian photographers.

2 iniva, the Institute of International Visual Arts, was founded in 1994.

3 For more information about black British photography, see *Ten.8*'s 'Critical Decade' issue, Spring 1992, and Creative Camera CC332.

20

Every Photograph Has a Story

Dawoud Bey photographed Stuart Hall at the National Portrait Gallery (NPG), London, during the former's short residency there. The diptych consists of unique Polacolor photographs created with a 20"x 24" Polaroid camera, one of only five ever made. The residency was produced in collaboration with Autograph ABP and the Barbican Art Gallery in 1998. Prior to his arrival in the UK, Dawoud Bey had asked me if I thought Stuart Hall would be prepared to have his portrait taken. I agreed I would try to get Stuart come to the NPG for a sitting. Stuart agreed and we met around lunchtime on Charing Cross Road just outside the Gallery. Stuart's son Jess Hall came along, as he was keen to see this unique machine in action.

The focus of Dawoud's residency was to work with a group of teenagers. The residency project was part of an ongoing project Dawoud was undertaking that questioned the representation of young people. When we arrived, Dawoud was just finishing off photographing a young Asian teenager and we quietly watched as he set about the task of making his images. Watching the large Polaroids appear was very intriguing, the direct and instantaneous nature of the Polaroid camera's function addresses all the qualities central to the alchemy of photography.

Stuart was invited to sit in a chair in front of the camera, which was very close. The overall scene was intimate, almost like an exchange of gifts. Dawoud said very few words but directed Stuart through a series of poses that shifted Stuart's gaze and head position both directly at the lens and away from it. Each time an image was peeled away from the body of the camera it was quickly hung on the wall to dry fully. I knew immediately that these images were special. I think less than ten photographs were taken and within the hour the session was over. My only narcissistic regret is that I never asked to have a photograph taken at this moment with Stuart. However, I take great pleasure in having played a small part in enabling these beautiful photographs of Stuart Hall to be created.

This text originally appeared in Cultural Studies, *Volume 23, Issue 4, 2009.*

Between Feeling and Time:
Brent in the 1980s and 1990s

It was 1991 when I first encountered Roy Mehta's photographs from Brent. Mehta generously permitted Autograph to use a small selection of the work in its newsletter-type publication. Earlier that same year, some of these photographs were exhibited at what was then the Watershed Media Centre in Bristol. The main focus of the work was the notion of faith within and across the diverse community of Brent.

Back then, Mehta's photographs seemed to work on the temporality of vision. This is because as images they seem to be locked in a double bind, caught up in the past and very much alive in our present. The photographs therefore function as calling cards to the way we were and ask us to reflect on what we have become. They work as powerful agents that challenge us to push back at time. They save us from the chaos of always moving on. They also do other important cultural work since they function as critical signs of kindness and acceptance. Mehta's work is a conversation being framed and across this series, his subjects respond with an openness that emits the tenderness of familiarity. These photographs therefore celebrate the intimate and tactile nature of human relationships – they are calming reminders of what closeness can look like.

Mehta's photographic praxis is grounded in a search for those elusive emotional states that make us, many of which will never be seen but, when looking with generosity, may well be felt. The dynamic that Mehta brings to his way of looking helps us remember that silence has great value and that being at peace within oneself is a fragile state that has to be valued and cared for with urgency. These photographs, as an offering to a community, invite us to share the atmosphere of a subject's inner being. They are charged with signs of care, compassion and faith. It's these three important elements that hold this body of work together. They are visible here as signs made manifest through gesture, style and cherished objects.

What emerges through the making of these photographs is an understanding of what is shared within a community rather than what divides it: healing and embracing, taking the pain of the daily strain away through touch; participation; waiting, holding and watching; being nourished through companionship and community. The strength of Mehta's Brent photographs is that they help us understand just how fragile we are. I hold these photographs dear because I locate them within a time of cultural and political solidarity with the subjects being framed. It's a sensation that I hope won't go away and that resists being consigned to memory because the importance of this photographic work is that it allows us to feel.

This text first appeared in Revival: London 1989-1993 *by Roy Mehta, published by Hoxton Mini Press in 2020.*

22

On John Goto

It is both a regret for not living in that past state of grace and a desire to recapture it. And against all intruders, all those strangers who threaten to tarnish or obstruct the enactment of promised communion, however illusionary it might be, there is recourse to a familiar violence. In that moment, one comes face to face with the scapegoat.

Albert Memmi

John Goto's portraits fill an important gap in our understanding of the way things were for young black British people in the 1970s. They offer an important counter-narrative, turning the tables on the historically dominant media image of black youth in Britain, which during the 1970s was mainly framed as wildly delinquent, to be feared and policed with intensity.

There was not enough 'mob' to be violent; the sight of murder and destruction put off as many as it inspired, while the overwhelming majority preferred to close their eyes and plug their ears, but first of all gag their mouths ... Racism is a policy first, ideology second. Like all politics, it needs organization, managers and experts.

Zygmunt Bauman

Goto's subjects do not form part of a journalistic story aimed at recording the day-to-day struggles of migrant life. There is no decisive moment here. The subjects sit quietly in cool anticipation of the shutter's release. Neither do these photographs work within the tradition of the high-street photographic studio: no bizarre fabricated backdrops have been used to create an imagined subject; there are no modern props; no phones without cables; no fake countryside to pose in front of. Therefore, it is what is absent from the photographs which makes them so compelling. The subjects are stripped away from the 'normal' conditions of reception. Maybe Goto put away these photographs for so long because at the time of their making the work had no place to go, no possible or meaningful home.

No image could act alone, of course. No image could, by itself, change the world, for every visual representation is dependent on context: the words, circumstances, distribution, and beliefs that endow pictures with greater levels of meaning and influence.

Maurice Berger

Goto's work is a radical photographic act, performed with his camera and a makeshift studio. This radical act, though relatively simple in its construction, elevates his sitters out of the visual noise by which they have been historically marked. To frame these individuals as classical subjects, on the eve of a night out in 1977, slows down our reception of them as a people always on edge, allowing us to see them not in crisis but in a tender exchange with themselves and the photographer. There are no riots or demonstrations here, just pleasure in the pose and sincerity of the relationships. The subject being placed at the centre of attention in a respectful and friendly environment means these images resist the weight of oppression.

Long refused access to honorific depiction, black bodies were confined to the frames of the criminal, the pornographic, the ethnographic, the comedic photograph, or to the margins of sentimental portraits of whites.

Leigh Raiford

What Goto's photographs do is imbue his subjects with a sense of formal importance, something that at the time of their making was clearly lacking in representations of black life, causing us now to pause and reflect on these difficult times.

I am invisible, understand, simply because people refuse to see me. Like the bodiless heads you see sometimes in circus side-shows, it is as though I have been surrounded by mirrors of hard, distorting glass. When they approach me they see only my surroundings, themselves or figments of their imagination, indeed, everything and anything except me.

Ralph Ellison

The images now perform a kind of visual democracy; they generate a sense of closeness that allows the language of intimacy, tenderness and participation to emerge, which was a rare achievement when we consider how black people had been framed.

2013

23

Masterji: The Photographs
of Maganbhai Patel

Western scholars working in photography have been culturally blinded by their own reflections. Rather than
acknowledging photography as being, from its inception, a truly
global phenomenon, Eurocentric curators and historians have
focused on building a photographic visual regime that places the
West above the rest.

What is evident once we pick over the remains of photography's
Eurocentric nature is that photography is haunted by its own colonial psyche. Reading the history of European photography in the
present tells us much more about the colonising eye than it does
about the myriad foreign Others it has focused on.

The old history of photography is now read as a fragmented and
broken body. It is a history full of missing chapters, absent stories,
lost, neglected and overlooked archives. It is therefore pressing
and urgent that photographic moments produced by the Other –
marginalised or historically colonised peoples – are brought out of
the archive and into the world. It is these images that help us in the
present to identify or close the historical cultural gaps that imperial
photographic regimes have imposed across our visual understanding
of the world.

It is only since the celebrated 1994 Bamako Photography Festival
that photography's Other histories began to enter Europe's cultural
institutions in any meaningful way. The distinguished Malian
studio photographers Seydou Keïta and Malick Sidibé have now
entered photography's great halls of fame. 1994 and the events in
Bamako mark the beginning of a decolonial history surfacing out of
photography.

These Other photographic histories are clearly diasporic and multifaceted in nature. What is compelling about these Malian and Other studio photographic practices, such as those of Suresh Punjabi who founded Studio Suhag in Nagda, a small town in India, is that the photographs produced there reside both within and outside of European photographic epistemic systems. Importantly, they require local knowledge to interpret their meanings fully, and as archives they reflect the outcomes of global human exchanges and encounters.

Critically, what is required for us to fully appreciate photography's Otherness is a new politics of reconstruction,[1] leading to alternative ways of thinking and seeing photography. Doing this will aid us in understanding the significance of and meanings produced when photography's missing chapters are brought forth out of obscurity and into the domain of representation.

Photography's history has been waiting for Maganbhai (Masterji) Patel's work to surface. The idea that from within the migrant body of Indian subjects journeying to Britain there was no one taking up the camera to document the hopes, dreams and aspirations of the newly arrived migrants to England marks a fault line in our under-standing of the global appeal of photography. More importantly, perhaps, what is revealed is the migrant desire to capture, through photography, their new sense of being. These photographs were sent home as a record of the subject having 'made it', not only to a new destination but having 'made it' as modern subjects in the modern world, framed within their own terms as uniquely future-facing people, with new and exciting identities.[2] What we must acknowl-edge is that, as future-facing people, they now had the capacity to generate and circulate their own new images, purely for pleasure.

Masterji's photographic practice is unique in the sense that he was clearly a photographer in tune with his people's sense of time and place. In picking up the camera to record this hugely transi-tional moment in both British and Indian history, what we can read is that Masterji considered himself and his family to be as much a part of this historical moment as the subjects he photographed. There is no great objectifying distance in Masterji's practice. He is culturally in love with his subjects. His sitters become a portrait of an extended family that are bound together not through bloodlines but through the lens of Masterji's camera. Masterji's photographs can therefore be read as intimate and quiet moments that operate between the internal and external desires of the subject in focus. It is in these moments that Masterji's studio becomes a laboratory for future thoughts in which both the real and the imagined self can emerge anew into the world.

This text was originally published as the foreword to Masterji *(Wonderful Books, NL, 2017).*

NOTES

1   Stuart Hall, 'Reconstruction Work: Images of Post-War Black Settlement', *Ten.8*, No. 16, 1984, pp2-9.
2   *Ibid.*

24

The Triumph of Optimism

The history of photography is full of missing chapters, suitcases of images waiting to be opened and archives in distress lying in filing cabinets, waiting for cultural agents to enunciate their worth.[1] When new archival photographic works surface that help us to understand our sense of place across both time and space, they engage us on a deeply personal, cultural and political level. What we experience is who we once were.

Syd Shelton's photographs, taken from 1976-81, offer a visual index of Britain as a house divided across race, class and gender. His work enables us to feel the ferocity of cultural difference being hammered out on Britain's streets. Through Shelton's images, one can see the steely determination of those who could no longer tolerate the archaic dullness of British society and its inherent inequalities.

Shelton's photographic archive provides us with a way into one of the most intriguing and contradictory political periods in post-Second World War British history, a time when racist skinheads danced to Jamaican ska, punks embraced reggae and black kids reached out to punk.[2] Meanwhile, disaffected white Britain turned to right-wing politics and a shopkeeper's daughter, Margaret Thatcher, became the Prime Minister.

However, the triumph of optimism across various cultural alliances would be epitomised by the events that took place in Lewisham, South London, on 13 August 1977, when a variety of different left-wing groups and community activists joined together to resist a major National Front march (Lewisham in the mid 1970s was a hotbed of racial tension).[3]

This period of Shelton's work marks an intriguing, fragile and volatile political moment that literally changed the world. This intense shift during the 1970s represents the prelude to Thatcher's most powerful moment, her second term, when she and Ronald Regan partnered in a political dance that would have us all 'rocking' to the beat of ideological conflict for years to come.

2012

NOTES

1 A. Sekula, 'The Body and The Archive' in *October*, No. 39, 1986, pp3-64.
2 The Clash, *Westway to the World*, DVD, 2001.
3 Lindsay Mackie, 'The real losers in Saturday's battle of Lewisham', www.theguardian.com/uk/1977/aug/15/race.world, 15 August 1977.

Experiments
with Time

25

From Here to Eternity (1999)

From Here to Eternity is the name of a photographic series produced by Sunil Gupta. The work was commissioned by Autograph, then the Association of Black Photographers, and was first shown at Standpoint Gallery, London. In 2020, Autograph published a book of Gupta's work by the same name.

Mark Sealy: 1999 is the point where *From Here to Eternity* is made, is that correct?

Sunil Gupta: That's right, yes.

MS: So, in 1999, where were you within the world of making photography?

SG: I was at rock bottom because I had some health episodes which made me take some time off. Because I was freelance, taking time off meant I didn't really have much income. I was signing on [to social security], it was a chicken and egg existence ... there was less and less money and less and less possibilities. Also, there was a short period when my health was such that I couldn't really go out myself. People had to come and walk the dog, bring groceries ... I became very dependent for a while. The outlook wasn't great at that point, you know. It was time to start from scratch.

MS: Two years into New Labour [elected 1997], there is a certain sense of social optimism around with things changing, especially in the first term of the New Labour government. There was a sense that people wanted to move past the old Labour type conversations. It's as if the socialist Left had become marginalised because for anybody who aligned to the values of the old Left, it seemed your time was over. New Labour had arrived and 'Cool Britannia' seemed to be on top of the world.

SG: Yes, I had also made a very big investment in curating, with that OVA-franchise for iniva.[1] My 1990s started on a high, I got this extraordinary grant that pulled me out of teaching, which I had thought was a good thing back then. My weekly commute to Hull would be no more and I could work from home. It was an exciting project, the idea of it. With the three of us, Eddie Chambers, Rasheed Araeen and me, I thought there was something to work with.

MS: The iniva franchises were a very bold move from the Arts Council of England, something that would grow really, wasn't it?

SG: This was 1992, before iniva had hired full-time people. We did our own thing and there was a very supportive atmosphere around it, from the Arts Council and the funders. People were very receptive and because I had a budget given to me in advance … it really changed my game. People in key positions in the art world now, who themselves were freelance then, would call me up and say, 'Can I work with you?' I had the money, you know?

MS: It's amazing what money does in terms of new friends.

SG: Yeah. The mid 1990s was a peak moment, it turned around my fortunes a bit. iniva got going and the staff got hired, then there was the Havana Biennale in 1995, where I was showing as an artist. I went out there in the company of the new Director.

MS: It [iniva] became very administrative … institutionalised as an Arts Council client.

SG: Yeah, institutionalised. I didn't join and consequently I lost my budget, and then I was on my own. I turned around to the Arts Council and said, 'I'm just going to keep applying as a freelancer, keep the company going that way, on project grounds'. So that's what I did, but that became much tougher because it was harder to make longer-term programming plans.

MS: Everything was dependent on the success of an application, like an annual revenue mountain to climb. You had to apply for funding every year and there was every chance you were not going to get it. That was a constant threat at Autograph as well, a never-ending cycle of proving your worth. In short, 1992-94, those are what I would call the 'franchise years', where your making process became secondary and the curatorial process became primary.

SG: Yes, I completely dropped editorial work. I never worked for Fleet Street or anything.

MS: There was a kind of 'artist meets curator'. It's funny, isn't it … Eddie [Chambers] was an artist, Rasheed [Araeen] was an artist and you were an artist. There were these three men from very different access points now working directly with artists from non-Eurocentric perspectives. They were quite interesting and were key foundation blocks concerning iniva's development. What happened to your photography during this period?

SG: I did very little photography. Basically those chapters of *Trespass* were all triggered by something.[2] The first one was triggered as a commission from *Trophies of Empire*, the project from 1992. In 1994 and 1995 the other two were also triggered, one by a request from Frank Wagner at NGBK, Berlin, to be in a show, and one by the Focal Point Gallery, Southend. The commissions were between them and Essex County Council … that's why Part 3 is all in Essex.

MS: Yes, it might have been part of something called the Cross Channel Photographic Mission, wasn't it? That organisation was looking at the Britain's relationship across the English Channel as a response to the Channel Tunnel opening. Anne McNeill, the current director of Impressions Gallery in Bradford, was key in that development and it went on to become Photoworks UK, which is now based in Brighton.

SG: She might have been, but the woman that was running the Impressions Gallery, York, back then was called Cheryl Reynolds.

MS: That's right.

SG: She had taken over Impressions from Paul Wombell, who had moved on to direct the Photographers' Gallery in London.

MS: Cheryl Reynolds, I remember. We did a few things with the Impressions when Cheryl was there. She was open to conversations. In 1995, Cheryl helped us do the Rotimi Fani-Kayode exhibition titled *Communion* at Impressions. The Cross Channel Photographic Mission was a small photography organisation based in the southeast of the UK, trying to build relationships across the channel or look at the new regulations coming in place around the EU. There was a lot of focus around the EU again in the 1990s … immigration was very much in focus. That story, it seems to me, hasn't changed for a very long time … about the fear of people coming in, 'swamping' Britain. I think the Channel was seen as a portal for a possible invasion from Europe.

SG: That's how I approached it, Essex as a gateway to the UK.

MS: It's fair to say that by the time you picked up the camera to do *From Here to Eternity*, you're not in a good place. The curating has stopped, funding has dried up, old photography clients have been dropped, you're not working for an organisation and all of a sudden you are diagnosed with a major illness: HIV.

SG: Yes. This kind of distance opened up between me and what used to be my home inside black arts. I was no longer seeing those people, I was no longer casually bumping into black artists anywhere. I fell out of all those networks.

MS: I think what happens when you become a grantee is that the relationship changes with people because suddenly you are someone to hustle rather than a hustler.

You and I met in 1986-87. Something changed around 1999. I remember talking to you and sensing instinctively that you were not in a good place, that things weren't right. I think you said something like, 'I want to make work again'. You might have showed me one or two of these pieces you had been doing. I always knew you as a photographer so it was a case of, how do we get this process of making work going again?

I was very mindful that the HIV conversation was somehow falling off the agenda in terms of public awareness and it was quite important for you to address public and private life side by side. I was very interested in that; I was very interested in places where people were still engaging with each other and how AIDS was just being ignored. The gay nightclub scene was still very alive, but the impact of HIV was being internalised, it seemed. I was interested in the honesty of the way you used your body, your relationship to the body, the mirror, degrees of reflection, and these spaces of containment and desire represented in the nightclubs.

SG: I think the first picture was a random one, as often happens with me, and it became the basis for it, the one of the mirror and just my body holding up the camera. That camera came back into use, it was my editorial camera which I didn't use anymore ... digital had come. I just put some colour film into it, this is the old Hasselblad, and I used that in a hotel room, hand held. This was very accidental, almost like a phone selfie, but because it was 120 and a Hasselblad, it became more than a selfie through that medium format process.

I think you are right about what you are saying. My underlying conclusion from the diagnosis, which in the early years I thought was *death is around the corner* kind of thing, *time is running out,* made me think about what is of value in one's life, what are you doing? I thought, all this arts admin I'm doing, writing emails to people, who really cares about all that? I really need to make more pictures and less curating. I was tied to the curating as income, so I was caught in a bit of a trap. It was dwindling and I was sensing pressure from the Arts Council. People like me were gradually moving away and they began to tell me to really narrow my focus onto Asian artists.

MS: I also think that, internally, once 1994 had happened, with the institutionalisation of part of the blacks arts scene in the UK, the funders were saying, 'That's all the money for you lot, it's all over there now. Don't come here for more support'. These are the things I used to talk to Stuart Hall about, and he was very mindful that there was a danger of homogenisation in having one institution that was supposed to speak to all of the issues concerning diversity in the arts. It was clear that only one organisation that looked at diversity could exist in the Arts Council's mind, only one organisation could be prioritised.

The idea of Autograph – I was told directly by people – was irrelevant now that these changes had happened. Smaller, grass-roots organisations were seen as too local and not global. They had become much more vulnerable in this climate.

Looking at *From Here to Eternity*, if we are going to use your life in politics around the black arts as a framing, it is a very fragile moment, it's not in good shape.

SG: No, it's waning …

MS: It's about how we survived that space and time. I do not think people realise how precarious it all was. Hanging on as a way of being was so stressful on every level. When I look at the photographs you produced, 'Shroud' and 'The Pleasure Dome', which are key images from the series 'From Here to Eternity', it's almost as if the idea of pleasure is dead.

SG: Yes, there was a dismantling of stuff around me that happened very fast in the 1990s. A company [OVA] at the beginning of the 1990s with several key people passing away, one after the other, it was crazy. There were the deaths and people who shrugged their shoulders and walked away. Some people just said, 'I'm moving to Margate, don't bother calling me, I'm done with this'. So I did feel it was waning a bit.

MS: In retrospect, it seems as if the sector courted the conversations outside of the local. 'Elsewhere' became the go-to point of reference, everyone was chasing that kind of space as if that was the golden chalice, the holy grail. People seemed to be leaving the sector physically and spiritually. There was something out there in the international world that was being chased, and lots of things locally were being left behind in terms of the politics of state support.

SG: My local scene shrank. At one point it was just Joy Gregory ... I barely saw the other black artists in London for a while. I think that made me sit up and think about my work.

MS: In 1999, I had been working at Autograph for eight or nine years. I felt it was a weird time because it was as if a major chapter had ended. The new century was coming, some people were becoming very, very famous through their work, with shows in major institutions, which was great. Yinka Shonibare was on the rise, Chris Ofili, Steve McQueen, mainly men actually. It seemed as if artists were becoming either disenfranchised or corporatised.

Galleries were opening and becoming incredibly powerful, there were big private spaces, there was lots of money around it seemed and yet somehow if you were not on that gravy train, if you didn't get picked up, you would be dropped and called marginal. The Arts Council seemed to be led by *Frieze* magazine, Art Angel and the Serpentine ... it was all heading towards blue chip, whereas underneath all of that were a lot of people wondering how to navigate it all. It was that moment when curators turned up in designer wear ...

SG: Producers ...

MS: Like TV or Hollywood executives.

SG: With a briefcase ...

MS: The briefcases came out and taxis were being hailed ... people were hanging out in Regent's Park, and Mayfair was on the rise again.

SG: That's true ...

MS: Groucho Club, Fred's or some other members' club was the destination if you were going be successful. It was no longer Brixton, it was back to the West End. And there you are, in a place of critical care. Medicines, drugs and isolation.

SG: Yes, that's true. I think this body image thing became very critical around gay male identity, where promiscuity and having the ability to attract people was paramount. You begin to feel like nobody will want to sleep with you anymore, and then the whole trauma of disclosing your HIV status. All these things become factors to keep you indoors. I began to go out less and less, even socially. And that's when I got the dog.

MS: Yes, then Babe arrived …

In the context of this conversation, if I look at clubs like Attitude and Pleasuredrome, it's interesting because in the photographs they are all closed, nothing is open in the daytime. They become symbolic of impenetrable forces of pleasure, and your drugs maintain a status quo of existence … but it's like, *existing for what?*

SG: Yes, that's true.

MS: I must admit, I thought that was a really bold way of thinking of one's place in a gay community, as such, or lifestyle. Having all of that taken away from you through alienation and through an erosion in confidence … and getting older and getting ill, and then excluded and caught in this limbo of not having financial or institutional support. It's a bit like being sacked for being you or having reached a sell-by-date.

SG: Yes, and it all happened around the age of 45. By my mid 40s I should have been getting somewhere … it was all removed suddenly.

MS: Were things happening in India?

SG: No, I hadn't been to India for a decade by then. I spent the 1990s not going to India. When I began doing the curating, I think I did one project out of India. I thought I'd go beyond India, I worked with a couple of artists from Southeast Asia; I worked with Australian, Canadian and South African artists.

MS: The Commonwealth …

SG: Yes, settler colonies … I made a sideways move very easily, nobody asked any questions. I went from little brother photography into the art world, and I was saying: 'The history of landscape painting in the nineteenth century, blah, blah, blah, let's put Durban together with Melbourne, together with Toronto ... they all have their Victorian painters. Let's see what contemporary painters make of that history.' That's what I did, and everyone said, 'Wow!' That also came from meeting people ... I met Stan Douglas in a gay bar because he was a DJ in Vancouver, and not because I thought he was some great artist.

MS: That's great.

SG: I feel you have to go out and put yourself out there.

MS: That sense of fluidity as well, and the boundaries between the making and the being. Being in it, being in the scene ... lovers and conversations. I think people get confused, there are lots of conservative notions about how we make and who we are, and where consensual relationships begin and end in those conversations.

SG: Yes.

MS: Babe seemed to be a way of getting out ... walking the dog.

SG: Yes, gets you out twice a day, as you know now.

MS: But I thought the funniest pairing in this work was Babe and then Fist [laughs] ...

SG: [laughs]

MS: I mean the idea of pairing a dog with a gay bar called Fist [laughs] ... And then that Indian landscape, somewhere in frame ... there is a tower beside it and an arch. There you are, holding Babe, and there's this tower and arch.

SG: Oh, yes! It's a famous nineteenth-century picture by Bourne and Shepherd of the Qutb Minar in Delhi.

MS: It feels as if it has that classical Indian architecture thing and then you there and this phallic pole behind you and Babe [laughs].

What is nice about this work is that serendipity arrives in many parts of it. I think some of the best things are being made in the unconscious. Obviously, that is not a chance moment, it's a very deliberate act of tenderness. Against the stigma of HIV – to root AIDS back to its early journalistic days, it was God's punishment … a gay plague. These narratives underpin all of these questions and media phobias.

How did you come up with the title, Sunil?

SG: I was thinking of the movie *From Here to Eternity*, which is based on a book. It's post-war and they were doing the nuclear tests in the South Pacific. It was kind of about that Cold War pessimism … 'we are on the verge of being blown up'. In fact, I since realised that the title itself came from a poem by Rudyard Kipling. Believe it or not, it was written about the last British soldiers who came out of Afghanistan back in the nineteenth century. He wrote, 'and here they are, from here to eternity'. There is a famous painting about a similar moment at Tate that was displayed during that exhibition that focused on colonial painting, *Artist and Empire*. Curiously, a reproduction of it also appears in one of the *Lovers: Ten Years On* portraits on the background wall.

MS: Yes, from 2015.

SG: There was this big painting of a horse in Afghanistan, a single horse with one guy on it. He was the last remaining English patrolman coming back, everybody else had been wiped out.

MS: That circles back to the current situation, right?

SG: Yes, absolutely. When I keep hearing all of this about the Taliban – people don't understand … when you are living there, they are your people. They don't want Americans telling them what to do. For better or worse, they are their own people.

MS: I do remember the movie …

SG: Up the Khyber Pass?

MS: [laughs] ... *Carry On up the Khyber* ... No, I mean the movie with Burt Lancaster, who is having an affair with the general's wife. It's called *From Here to Eternity* as well ... again, something going which shouldn't be going on, pleasure repressed. There is the great scene when they are embraced on the beach, in the waves, but they are not meant to be ...

SG: Yes, him lying on the beach in trunks looking sexy, Burt Lancaster with Deborah Kerr or someone.

MS: Debra Kerr, Frank Sinatra, and the pained Montgomery Cliff, who in this film is unbelievable. Frank Sinatra and the vicious Ernest Borgnine, who just beats the hell out of people... it's tragic.

It's such a poetic and loaded title, but it feels optimistic. We showed the work at the Standpoint Gallery in Hoxton. The East End was still possible to live in then, there were still studios for £3 per square foot. Things were possible. People could be mobile.

SG: Then White Cube arrived there suddenly.

MS: That's right ... right in the middle of Hoxton Square. And then it went, bang! We were in Hoxton Square next door watching this go up. And it was, 'Wow, how do we survive these blue-chip moments coming in?' We were around the corner from White Cube ... Jay Jopling, Damien Hirst in the window every day. And we were there, in complete antithesis to that moment. I think that's a good point you made, Sunil, because it felt they were never going to join the conversations, or we were never really going be allowed to speak in those types of spaces.

SG: Yes, I felt that by the end of that year, everything had been undone. The whole YBA ... what was that Blair thing about Britain called?

MS: Cool Britannia.

SG: Cool Britannia, yes, taking over …

MS: I think to talk about race and queer politics, feminism, and the working class … it just wasn't cool.

SG: I think some people thought all that was solved.

MS: I do believe there was a moment where even lots of black artists felt compromised.

SG: They didn't want to be black anymore, women didn't want to be women artists anymore. It was a liability on their way because everybody was trying to get up there.

MS: Everyone wants to be in the White Cube, as such. It's what success looked like.

SG: They didn't want to be taught by anything.

MS: I think there is a certain degree of amnesia around that time. History has been abstracted. I think lots of people are in denial about that period. I think that is a really good place to leave the making of *From Here to Eternity*, when the White Cube-isation of the scene became the overriding force that was pulling on people. It was depressing if you couldn't, or didn't, feel as though you were in the drag net of that development … and we certainly weren't. Things remained precarious.

NOTES

1 In 1992, Gupta established OVA: the Organisation for Visual Arts, a curatorial project. It was an Arts Council England-funded iniva franchise.

2 *Trespass* (1992-95) is a three-part photography project by Sunil Gupta.

Absence and Presence:
The Work of Oscar Muñoz

Photography is at its most intriguing when it generates a state of aesthesis: an unfettered awareness of stimulation. Recognising the sensorial experience offered by photography is radical because it frees the viewer from the confines of a purely Eurocentric aesthetic framing, opening up the space for sensing and perceiving the cultural work that a photograph does across different individual and cultural experiences.[1]

To consider the full complexities of the work photography does in contemporary visual culture, it needs to be addressed beyond the time of its production, the specifics of its geographical location, and outside the moments of its making. Doing so would allow for the production of different types of knowledge and understanding concerning the wider political temporalities in which a photograph has been produced. Critically, we have to drag photography away from postmodern narratives that dominate how we analyse the work photography has done across visual culture. The photographic work of Oscar Muñoz is crucial to this endeavour.

Muñoz's practice agitates against cultural amnesia, bringing into awareness the lost histories of the voiceless, the disappeared and those trapped within a 'state of exception'.[2] The 'state of exception', as described by Giorgio Agamben, represents the condition whereby a sovereign state acts violently on an individual life from outside the established norms of the law. This creates a social order where the individual becomes disempowered and exposed to ephemeral being, living a transient life that is in turn made politically non-existent, with catastrophic consequences. At the heart of Muñoz's photographic art is the reminder that modern democratic states have the capacity to turn into horrific totalitarian regimes with ease.

Photographic images work in unique ways on individual human subjects. There is no universal or decisive moment concerning a photographic encounter because the matrix of an image's reception is culturally fluid. The reception of an image cannot be dictated by its designated 'punctive' moments.[3] The generation of meaning from within a photograph is not fixed, as it forms part of a conjuncture with our experiential being. However, human subjects in different times and cultural spaces see things differently. Each time we see an image, it cannot be as it was before because we as viewers have changed in time. Photographic images themselves can only be understood within the contexts of the different temporalities and cultures within which we apprehend them or to which they relate, and only once we understand the cultures within which an image is read can we begin to lock down any meaning produced by that image.

Reading the archive of photography's past as fixed significantly constrains any understanding of the myriad possible meanings archive photographs produce in the present. The establishment of a canonical reading of photography and photographic epistemologies is a decidedly European affair and is in no way universal or democratic. European epistemologies operate in other, often dark ways across the lived experiences of people.

The experience of photographic time and the fixing of history for those who live in conditions of oppression and violence, state or otherwise, works as a form of disavowal – a denial of freedom. This is distinctly different from the experience of those who enjoy freedom and the luxury to imagine. If we, as human subjects, have nothing to look forward to, then photographic time is a prison, a concentration camp, a slaver's boat, a refugee holding centre, a debased, unknown black body, a framed subject that cannot come into being. Photographic time traps the disenfranchised into an image life sentence. Photography for those locked out of the means of image production becomes an impossible barrier to the right to full and equal human recognition, especially if existence alone is an act of survival and the image of an unrecognised life is one of cultural stagnation.

As forms of intimate engagement, photographs, when read through different temporalities, have the capacity to make us feel much more than we actually see, and it's in the feeling of photographs that we can locate the practice of Oscar Muñoz. Muñoz operates beyond the dazzling and objectifying nature of a photograph. His practice works in the realm of the visceral, and at the centre of his work lies a series of critical questions concerning empathy and the boundaries of our human obligation to one another.

If we are allowed to consider a photograph to be something we feel, we can acknowledge critical photographic work as work that enables the different temporalities of our human pasts, presents and futures to surface. If we accept photographs as objects that help us to care for each other, then photographs offer us the unique opportunity to touch time, an act that makes us aware of the plasticity of our own consciousness.[4]

Photographs do their cultural work well when they agitate those Barthesian punctive moments that are uncontrollable and unknowable, producing charged synaptic exchanges in the viewer's memory formations. The visual recognition system of the brain resides in a region known as perirhinal cortex. Certain neurons in this area discriminate between objects that have not been seen before and those that have been seen recently. Within the perirhinal cortex, millions of images that have been seen before are lodged within the dark matter of our minds, lying dormant until a trigger, conscious or unconscious, disturbs an image's presence and reanimates the past to come forth and claim its place in the present. In photographic time, all images are ghosts. 'The photograph transports the photographed into the time and space of the viewer. To recognise this is to go mad, for ghostly traces become real, and present; they touch and haunt the viewer'.[5] It's within the realm of the spectre that Muñoz's work can be aligned to the theoretical positions of Barthes; they both champion a kind of disruptive visual, grasping for madness.

Photography as a process not only captures time – the moment of an image capture – but looking at photographs also frees us from our sense of self as we become absorbed in the subject observed. Photography, as Muñoz is fully aware, has the capacity to breathe life into the process of our memory formation. Photography slows us down as well as drives us forward. Photography as a rear-view mirror on humanity helps us understand the way we were and what has passed.

Photography's capacity to connect us to our sense of being makes it an invaluable visual pathway for embracing the subject presented, allowing one's self to be touched without demanding 'reference or representation'.[6] Muñoz's practice is therefore uniquely located because, as visual forms of enquiry, his work creates the space for unexpected thoughts and feelings to surface into our present consciousness. How, who and what do we remember? What is it we are calling back into existence through photography and memory? And where does memory take us?

Muñoz's *Ambulatorio* (2012) is a floor-based installation made up of thirty-six, large-scale aerial photographs. These photographs are presented as panels, covered with sheets of security glass that break under the weight of the audience as they walk over the work, heads bowed in scrutiny of what lies beneath. Bowing one's head as a form of human exchange within different cultures conveys expressions such as apology, gratitude, humility, respect or remorse. Here, *Ambulatorio* commands the audience to bow their heads in recognition of our collective responsibility for each other, the burden of our human condition and our pasts.

Ambulatorio invites its audiences to participate in making the past real in the present by addressing what Judith Butler terms the 'ungrievable lives'[7] of people designated as 'disappeared'. It does this by positioning the audience on and above the work in a power relation that makes the viewer literally look down into the space of violence that historically frames cities such as Cali in Colombia and Belfast in Northern Ireland. Both these cities have been traumatised by conflict and the lives of many have been shattered as a consequence of decades of violence.

Walking on *Ambulatorio* is a cautious, unnerving and disturbing affair, as when walking over the work the viewer begins to realise that they are contributing to the further shattering of the glass, which would, in normal circumstances, be used to protect the photographic works displayed. The normal order of viewing objects in this moment is subverted. The breaking of glass becomes symbolic of a dysfunctional nation state that does not, or will not, protect its citizens, and the consequent vulnerability of justice within these societies.

By walking onto the work, the viewers have entered the domain of unknown, fragile existences and discomforting, unheard narratives that seek but fail to find justice through the rule of law. To add further to this condition of fragility and anxiety, the viewers have to look down through the broken glass to see into the city, hanging their heads as if out of shame for their inability to act on behalf of those who have been caught up in the violence of these unresolved pasts. It's at this point of engagement that the viewer begins to understand that all representation is breakable and not fixed. In the act of breaking the glass and looking down onto the shattered city, the viewer's own ruinous capacity is brought to bear.

Ultimately, then, the audience is aligned with the latent destructive forces present within the work. The acknowledgement of their own privileged position as voyeurs is made evident through their physical encounter with the work. The tactile process of crushing the glass reproduces the power of authoritarian rule that is addressed within the work. Here the audience is a player in the making of fragmented and violent histories, and the clarity they seek through the work becomes harder and harder to find since the more they survey the scene, the more obscure it becomes. Finding an image becomes a forensic process fraught with difficulty, which echoes the experience of those seeking justice within an unjust state. In this moment the city becomes an increasingly unrecognisable zone, as with each step in trying to understand the work, the audience releases shards of the unrecognised histories contained within the cities' violent pasts.

Ambulatorio as an installation disturbs the status-quo way in which photography and evocations of memory and violence work on the human subject. Here the silent encounter between the subject of death and the making of a memorialising object is unlocked. Engaging with *Ambulatorio* induces within the audience a fragile, vertiginous state of mind. With every step across the work the viewer shatters both the past and present, thus evoking a sense that history's critical moments reside in the deserted futures of unresolved conflicts.

The dialogic aspects contained within the work remind us that *Ambulatorio* is part of an active process of understanding the continued presence of violence in people's lives. *Ambulatorio* creates a dynamic interaction between memory and turbulent histories where thoughts and feelings combine to produce unique visual and sensorial experiences. An encounter with *Ambulatorio* reminds us all that our time in life's journey only needs an unfortunate moment to be irreparably broken, and that our capacity to be empathic towards each other needs to be nurtured at all times.

Muñoz's work worries the space of official records and memorials concerning violence. Through another work, *Aliento* (1995), he offers the viewer a visual gambit that provokes questions concerning the life of images. It's a provocation that asks us to consider the relationship between breath, *aliento*, and sight.

Aliento is made up of a series of portraits individually printed onto highly polished, reflective steel discs. The portraits are created by applying a grease photo-silkscreen process to the discs that makes the printed image invisible to the naked eye. Hauntingly, buried within these reflective surfaces are the faces of deceased Colombians who have been 'disappeared'. To be 'disappeared' is to experience a violent political act of killing or kidnapping. It is most often associated with oppressive regimes that brutalise those they see as being a threat to power, either politically or culturally. Muñoz has gathered his 'disappeared' subjects from the obituary pages of Colombian newspapers.

To make the image visible, viewers have to breathe directly onto the reflective surface of the disc. The invisible portraits can only emerge via the condensation that is produced by the viewer's breath when it touches the steel disc. The punctive drama and reception of the image is not produced solely through the act of seeing; *Aliento* demands a more complex bodily engagement from the viewer, drawing out a sensorial relationship to the subject as it effectively commands audiences to give the images the 'kiss of life'.

In breathing onto the disc, the viewer obscures their own reflected image and renders visible the subject who is 'officially' no longer present. The viewer's breath aids a fleeting resurrection for those who are lost and unable to be claimed – those marked as 'disappeared'. The most cruel and disturbing aspect of the process of 'disappearances' is that the families affected are left with no physical body to mourn and put to rest, and so are unable to obtain closure. To be 'disappeared' means bequeathing those left behind a state of emotional turmoil, living in the desperate hope that, one day, their loved ones may return.

Through *Aliento,* Muñoz has produced a radical photographic work that acts as a form of image and subject resurrection. It's through the viewer's own breath that the image enters their consciousness and, as they struggle to maintain the presence of the subject, they in turn become responsible for the subject's presence or absence. The struggle for the viewer to keep the image visible aligns them to the families of those who have been 'disappeared'. The physical act of breathing onto the work in order for the subject to have a visual life draws the viewer into an unending act of responsibility for keeping the photographic image of the victims alive in the present. Muñoz is aware of the impossibility of this task, but by inviting us to engage with *Aliento* what he asks us to do, through our own breath, is to give life not just to the subject framed within the work, but also to the idea that we are all, in a humanitarian sense, responsible for every single person that has met death by unlawful violence, state or otherwise. The images that surface in *Aliento* through our breath therefore function as cultural signposts that point towards a form of political haunting, a haunting that calls on us all to keep giving oxygen to the fight against social and political injustice.

Línea del Destino (*Line of Destiny,* 2006) also represents a quest to unearth empathy for violent episodes that have slipped through the gaps of history. The work carries on Muñoz's (unachievable) mission to hold back the tide of forgetting.[8] The work is a two-minute, silent, single-channel, black-and-white video. The opening sequence presents a slightly cupped hand holding a small amount of water as if to drink. From within the shimmering surface of the silvery water, the face of a man slowly comes into focus, staring directly back at the viewer. As the face appears, we also are drawn to the fact that the surface area of the water and therefore the image is slowly diminishing as the water slips through the fingers of the cupped hand. The watery self-image that is draining away through the hand of the artist becomes symbolic of the vain quest to hold onto life.

Through *Línea del Destino* we are presented with a tragic sense of the human soul being emptied, dried up and lost forever. When water is present in the work of Muñoz it suggests that there is still hope, but as it evaporates or is allowed to drain away so too does this sense of optimism. *Línea del Destino* is in effect an anti-auto-portrait. In a disturbing impermanence, the face of the artist stares back at the viewer and then slowly slips away, along with the water that reflects it. The title of the work references the practice of palmistry, which is the art of reading a person's character and future through the lines and patterns of their palms. By presenting his own disappearing image through the palm of his own hand, Muñoz shows us that he is conscious of his own fragile existence. For him, destiny is not shaped by fate alone. As for the majority of people, his fate is increasingly out of his own hands.

Línea del Destino reminds us that personal, cultural and political memory are fleeting, and that the fate of our future selves is not a pre-determined affair. Muñoz therefore offers his audience a dialogue around the question of how we exist in the face of violence. He asks us to consider the impact on our being when we are consistently subjected to actual political and cultural violence, or the threat of political and cultural violence, through a highly mediated world that is increasingly amnesic.

The use of the face in Muñoz's practice, whether it is his own or those of unnamed subjects, ultimately calls the audience to a place of responsibility for the Other. What's important for Muñoz is not that we recognise, in a literal sense, the face of the subject presented in his work; he is demanding more of us than reading the names and places of those that have suffered. Critically, what Muñoz is reminding us is that we are responsible for the face of the Other and that we have to care for all those unknown faces we have encountered. Without that core form of human recognition, he seems to suggest, humanity is doomed.

2018

NOTES

1   Walter Mignolo and Rolando Vazquez, 'Decolonial AestheSis: Colonial Wounds/Decolonial Healings', www.socialtextjournal.org/periscope_article/decolonial-aesthesis-colonial-woundsdecolonial-healings, 15 July 2013.
2   Giorgio Agamben, *Homo Sacer: Sovereign Power and Bare Life*, Stanford University Press: California, 1998, p83.

3 Roland Barthes, *Camera Lucida*, Hill and Wang: New York, 1981, p27.
4 'Brain Basics: The fundamentals of neuroscience', www.bris.ac.uk/synaptic/basics/basics-6.html, accessed 15 February 2022.
5 Shawn Michelle Smith, 'Race and Reproduction in *Camera Lucida*', in J. J Long, A. Noble and E. Welch (eds), *Photography: Theoretical Snapshots*, Routledge: London, p108.
6 *Ibid.*, p109.
7 Judith Butler, *Precarious Life: The Powers of Mourning and Violence*, Verso: New York, 2006, p148.
8 Laurel Reuter, *The Disappeared/Los Desaparecidos*, Charta: Grand Forks, 2006, p104.

27

Drowning World (2007-2018)
by Gideon Mendel

Through his project *Drowning World*, Gideon Mendel brings into sharp focus the catastrophic impact that global commerce has had on the ecologies that sustain life on Earth. For over a decade, Mendel has been recording and archiving the effects of flooding on the human condition. Rather than reproducing the visually tired depictions that flow from the mass of Eurocentric cameras capturing the world's disaster zones, saturating Western audiences with images of people in the global South framed on the edge of life, Mendel offers his viewers a critical turn within the documentary tradition through a body of work that brings the issue of global warming 'home'. Within this project, the personal and symbolic impact of flooding has become a more inclusive and democratic affair. It's no longer just about the wretched of the earth, it's about all of us. Time and space have closed the gap on the subjects rendered within the *Drowning World* project; the people in the photographs have become a unified, collective voice trying to be heard from within the pressure of rising waters.

Intimacy and fragility are the key visual signifiers that hold all the episodes of Mendel's *Drowning World* project together. This is done through the evocation of our shared exposure and vulnerability to the effects of global warming since none of us, independently, nationally or globally, can withstand the rising waters. The idea of turning back the clock on the effects of global warming is now undoubtedly a flawed proposition.

Mendel's photography agitates a sense of our failed responsibility for the environment, exposing ideologies of the Anthropocene that feel ever more present in a world eroded by international political inertia and a complete disregard for the health of the planet, and by extension the human subject. Mendel's *Drowning World* project demands to be read as a series of tragi-epic episodes that provoke the same question, again and again: who is responsible for protecting the Earth from human greed? The *Submerged Portraits* taken by Mendel make up the opening chapter of *Drowning World*. They are direct and intimate portraits of people living through the experience of floods. Their poses seem conventional but the unsettling gaze of the subjects challenges the viewer to consider their context and individual circumstances. Some, for example, present themselves as defiant and resilient people, the fight against the waters representing only a small part of their ongoing struggles to survive. The photograph of Adlene Pierre from Haiti has her framed within the doorway to her home, refusing to be cast as a victim. Instead, her gaze jabs at the viewer. She seems to be asking how much of this drowning world she is supposed to tolerate, and how many of her people have to drown, culturally, politically and environmentally, before the world acknowledges the value of her life?

For some of those photographed by Mendel, especially those subjects that have grown used to comfortable conditions of Western life, the trauma of their condition is evidentially unbearable. The presence of the camera thus becomes a moment in which to express their grief. The photograph taken of Terrence McKeen with his mother Gloria in Florida portrays them as though condemned to a submerged life, one where they must eternally reconcile the presence of rising waters.

Mendel's portraits work on the viewer as a form of judgment. They stir in us a fear that the waters are unknowingly and increasingly closer to all our front doors and that the exposure to the condition of flooding is no longer something that simply concerns those distant Others.

2018

28

Travelling Backwards:
The Mother of All Journeys (2007)

On a winter's day in 2001, the photographer/film-maker Dinu Li was busy helping his mother clean her house. While tidying things up, he realised just how few material objects she possessed. Though the house was of a reasonable size, it was, in fact, relatively sparse. Li's mother was born in rural south China. Once she had married, she moved to Hong Kong with her husband, where they raised a family. Then, in 1972, they decided to migrate to England.

The act of cleaning or cleansing (*katharsis*) on that winter's day in 2001 triggered in Li's mind an early childhood memory from Hong Kong when, in exchange for being told stories, he would tidy his mother's dressing table. The dressing table had a protective glass top and positioned underneath were an array of family photographs. These old family photographs were the source of the many stories Li's mother told him as a child, both factual and invented, stories that fuelled his early imagination and fired, in later life, his desire to become an artist. They also helped him understand his own direction of travel by helping him understand where he came from.

In feeling his way through both his own and his mother's memories, it became evident to Li that he needed to understand more of the story that his mother is. Once the housework was complete, Li and his mother agreed that they would travel back to China and journey through the stories of her life. Li's objective was to create a space where their memories might co-exist in time. Over their journey, Li produced a series of site-specific photographs from China, Hong Kong, Sheffield and Manchester. The newly made photographs, coupled with the diary-like notes of his mother, create visual and temporal leaps when brought into dialogue with the old family photographs. The work they managed to produce encourages the viewer to traverse back and forth across the landscape of Li's mother's memory.

Conceptually, the project offers the reader an opportunity to contemplate how a shared memory might work and how family archives function as contemporary agents that frame lives. The radical moment within *The Mother of All Journeys* (2007) as a visual conversation is how it sutures Li's mother's memories to his own. Through the physical act of journeying together, Li re-joins a lost past that he can now access independently, not as memories inherited but as memories made.

Dinu Li's decision to make an arduous journey with his mother, aimed at turning actual memories or stories into a lived and shared visual experience, is a complex psychological and physical process to endure. The need for children to tell their parents' story is a powerful desire. Most children get great satisfaction listening to family stories relayed to them by their parents, even if the stories change in some slight detail with each repetition. Eventually, the stories are deposited and become owned or translated in a different way, transforming into a new currency. It is understood that somewhere in the many different versions of the past, there is a variant 'truth,' mixed with a degree of exaggerated personal drama, depending on when, where and how a story is being told.

If we repeatedly return to an image or a story, it will change by the degree of our experience,

> hence the charm of family albums. Those grey or sepia shadows, phantom like and almost undecipherable, are no longer traditional family portraits but rather the disturbing presence of lives halted at a set moment in their duration, freed from their destiny; not, however, by the prestige of art but by the power of an impressive mechanical process: for photography does not create eternity, as art does, it embalms time rescuing it simply from its proper corruption.[1]

We bring more time and experience with each visit to a photographic object, while the object remains the same. Inevitably, we have new readings of the embedded image and see the same signs with a greater or lesser degree of clarity. New signs are observed as old signs are erased.

The old family photograph is a potential site of torment, constantly re-signifying and referring to a time before you either existed or can remember. The placing or depositing of the family archival photograph has not been your responsibility, it has been passed on along with other family baggage. The challenge is to try and make sense of the presence of personal history through the photograph before some of the key players disappear.

Trying to make meanings out of a family history through the photographic object is an ongoing process. It plays into the fantasy of being able to hold on to the past. Photography comfortably aids the desire to look into the past through its 'detachable nature, which allows it to refer to an absent object separated from it in space and time.'[2] It delays the fact of the departing. It pretends the past is present. It allows the viewer to imagine they have a fixed purchase on a transient set of images.

Dinu Li has chosen the most difficult way to travel: backwards. How many migrants of Dinu Li's mother's generation make the return journey home? Photographs are passed on and carried across the borders of personal memory, attended by narratives that, like the photographs themselves, are not fixed in meaning. Photographs reveal to us as much as we bring to them. The process of revisiting the past reveals more about the author in the present than about the subject in the past. When we recall a moment through an old photograph, meanings will always be constructed in the present, as we are only one part of the story.

This essay first appeared in The Mother of All Journeys *(Dewi Lewis Publishing, 2007), and was revised in 2021.*

NOTES

1 Andre Bazin, 'The Ontology of the Photographic Image', in Alan Trachtenberg (ed), *Classic Essays on Photography*, Leete's Island Books, 1980, p242.

2 Tom Gunning, 'Tracing the Individual Body: Photography, Detection, and Early Cinema', in Leo Charney and Vanessa R. Schwartz (eds), *Cinema and the Invention of Modern Life*, University of California Press: Berkeley, 1995, p20.

29

Waiting

There is a wonderful sense of calm about Youssef Nabil's photographs. It's the type of calm that says to the viewer, 'Nothing in this space is harmful.' Within the confines of Nabil's frames, there is a sense of security and pleasure. The photographs project an overriding message that says, 'It is right to love.' They speak to the vulnerable condition of desire, the risks of commitment and the fear of loss.

Nabil's photography consciously flirts with notions of the exotic and the erotic. The images slide seamlessly across a variety of different genres. They meld together to create a dreamlike mise-en-scéne. The photographs operate as visual narcotics, inviting the viewer into a place of transgressive otherness, a place that breaks with convention.

Nabil's visual web draws us into the land of fantasy and strategies for survival, for without dreams, we are doomed. His photographs have a resonance with Molina, the character in Manuel Puig's 1974 novel, *Kiss of the Spider Woman*. Nabil, like Molina, leaves us hanging on a thread of narrative tension. These photographs are loaded with a mood of quiet despair. They contain a sense of waiting that addresses a deep, underlying, personal-political message, which speaks to issues of desire and freedom. The luxury we have of looking at these images contrasts sharply with the reality of those who are forced to love in secret.

2007

30

Nothing Is Forever

I live with the image of death as part my daily consumption of news, films and an assortment of other media. I am never far from a television, so I see hear and read about endless violence and death. Rarely am I touched. Why should I be? It has nothing to do with me. It's entertaining, I'm happy with it.

The words 'distance' and 'family' must be related. 'Do I belong to a close family?' I've been asked that question many times. I lie and often say 'yes' when in fact I mean 'no'. In my past I've longed for closeness. Nothing is forever, it's a fact. That's the way I feel about relationships. In the end, something will always take someone away. Death is high on the removals list, along with desire and pride.

With that in mind, closeness is a relatively odd phenomenon. It's not necessarily physical closeness that matters, imagined closeness has a crucial role to play and is just as important. My fantasy of being close with a family member is in contrast to reality. It is difficult to be close to my family at the best of times, but I always desire it. I had anticipated that one day I would get closer to them (the family) – fat chance. I always assumed that there would be time. Not true. Time is always running out. There is no time left, only avoidance and large portions of guilt served up every time a family memory is evoked.

How, then, are you supposed to act when a parent dies? When my father died, a distant friend told me, 'There are only two kinds of people: those with parents and those without.' Peter Max Kandhola is without. Most people, in the course of their lives, will join him in that state.

Looking at death isn't difficult for me. Curiosity will always draw me to that which repulses or offends me, so I can find pleasure in other people's pain when it has been reconstructed for entertainment, sensationally presented for news or staged for art-world consumption. Together, art and gore are always winners, they're always controversial. Best value for money. Looking at the real dying is difficult, especially when not mediated by the usual channels.

The fact is that we're living with death all the time, though most of us are in denial. We simply cannot contemplate that the people we love most will, in fact, die. Maybe, if we're lucky, we might go first. Being left behind is tedious. I imagine what it's like to bury a child, imagine the roles reversed.

Over half million people in the UK will die every year.[1]

When a person is dying of cancer, they smell. I've smelled it. The combination of hospital antiseptic and internal rotting are very specific, especially if breathed on you as you attempt to get close to the dying. I desired distance when my father was dying. I fought real repulsion and shock for the first time. Who wants a close family if this is the result? What currency is there in relationships? Memory and loss have become photography's best friends. I can understand the need to photograph in such moments.

Someone said: 'Nowadays we die twice: first when we pass away, and the second time when no-one recognises us in a photograph.' I often write out lists of names because I have the impression that saying the name of someone brings them back to life for a few moments.[2]

As my father died, all of my instincts kept telling me to look away. Unlike Kandhola, who kept his lens focused on his dying father, I obeyed them. In the end, at the point of my father's death, I couldn't even make eye contact, let alone physical contact. Physical contact with those of my father's generation is hard at any time. Separated by an army of monitors, tubes and bags full of fluid (that somehow seemed to be simultaneously pouring stuff in and draining stuff out) was never going to make any meaningful contact easy. Too self-conscious. Uncomfortable. Blood, plasma, morphine, urine. Suspended plastic bags full of stuff. The presence of it all provided an array of interesting distractions. I remember how bizarre it seemed when my father used to move about the hospital with bags attached to various parts of his body to dispense drugs and collect various forms of waste. It was like watching the inside being out.

These body fluids, this defilement, this shit are what life with-stands, hardly and with difficulty, on the part of death. There, I am at the border of my condition as living being. My body extri-cates itself, as being alive, from that border. Such wastes drop so that I might live, until from loss to loss, nothing remains in me and my entire body falls beyond the limit – cadere, cadaver.[3]

How private, then, is death when a loved one dies in hospital? If you're lucky, you may have the seclusion of a closed room in which to contemplate bereavement and reconcile to your new situation. To get privacy on open wards, you're required to the pull curtains round the bed. Needless to say, you can hear and be heard with ease.

I protest about something. Demand attention because I can, but there's nothing that they can do because I'm not sure what I need.

The curtains around my father's bed were nylon. I hated even touching them.

Static, awful, plastic crap.

Patients make jokes to relieve their own tense, dire situation. I looked at them, the other dying people, a lot. I couldn't imagine how long they had left to live. I thought they could sense my enquiry, see it in my eyes, so I smiled and was compelled to look away. Simultaneously, I denied my own pathetic situation and somehow imagined that everything would return to 'normal' after the affair was over – not true.

You see signs of seepage when things fall apart. You can clock just how much fluid is around: the more fluid by the bedside, the more critical the situation. In hyper-clean environments, stains become more pronounced. The blemishes show up and attract one's atten-tion in an abnormal way. One is compelled to focus on the soiled details of the sanitised, depersonalised environment because it offers a visual distraction. One tries try to work out what exactly the stain might be. But whatever it turns out to be, rest assured – these are signs that the body is falling apart. You're looking at residue that may never be replaced.

The audio of the open ward can work as a welcome distraction when you experience death's cruel rattle. There is no last breath. It seems to take ages for a person to die in this manner. The end is often not a clean break but a struggle. I remember wishing it would all hurry up. Fallacious hope.

After I accepted Peter Max Kandhola's invitation to view his photographs of his dying father, I wasn't looking forward to the encounter. I really didn't want to enter into a dialogue on aesthetics and death and then offer practical advice about who, what and where to go with the 'work'. What's there to say? The capacity to offend is huge. I remember the irony of thinking, 'I hope the work is "good".'

It used to be appropriate to talk about issues relating to the image of death, but before, I had a distance from death. I was comfortable with it then. Now, following my own loss, I'm at ease with it in a different way. To be there at the point of death makes it different. Someone said to me that I was lucky to be there at the bedside of my father when he died. I knew what they meant, but 'lucky' was the wrong word – and yet I can't find one to replace it.

Peter Max Kandhola's work has been associated with death for some time. Those familiar with it will know that death is a theme he has visited on several occasions. His need to make this work does not come from a macabre compulsion to shock, but arrives from a desire to address the inevitable ending that most of us refuse to acknowledge. As his work progresses, it's not surprising that the intensity of his personal experiences take precedence. In this series of photographs we are forced to address our future and resign to our past.

Kandhola's photographs did not disturb me; in fact, they felt quietly familiar. They also made me jealous. At first, I found the work problematic simply because I didn't want to look. Now, after considering the images for some time, I find them comforting and tender. They have a therapeutic quality that enables you to imagine the moment of his father's death without experiencing too much pain.

If you can manage or digest the sense of loss that these photographs emanate then you can surface into a place that is ultimately celebratory and loving. Kandhola invites us to contemplate life through his experience of death in much the same way Bill Viola does in his celebrated work, *Nantes Triptych* (1992). Such work asks a very simple question: can we reconcile the fact that death is indeed part of life?

Kandhola's work marks the actual moment of his father's passing not in a romantic or dramatic way, but in a way that enables a degree of calmness and anticipation. Its non-theatricality is crucial to its success. Kandhola simply asks us to focus on the detail of his experience. The experience of death is nevertheless an awkward one. Awkward comes to mind because this project is, on the surface, loaded with discomfort. Its discomfort lies in the fact that we, the viewers of this very personal and everyday event, are invited to share the experience in a way that is not familiar. Of course, death for most people is unfamiliar.

In the hospital context, death is equated with failure. Consider Kandhola's father's body in its pre-death state, all it must have seen and done. Then consider his body as a post-death subject/object, about to be treated and prepared for final resting. The father becomes a site of contestation, confusion and a mass of assumptions and fears. All of a person's life struggles in this moment are being defined and lost, but hopefully also remembered. These photographs therefore have a key role to play in the act of reconciliation and the process of change. In such an intensive emotional situation, it is quite a profound and insightful act, to photograph.

In his ground-breaking CD-ROM project, *I Photograph to Remember*, the Mexican artist Pedro Meyer describes both his parents' battles with, and ultimate death from, cancer: 'I was so overwhelmed with my emotions that taking these pictures would enable me to someday understand'.[4] In 1986, the photographer Eugene Richards produced a compelling collaborative book with his long-time friend, Dorothea Lynch. *Exploding into Life* (1986) uses photography and diary entries to provide an insight into Dorothea Lynch's struggle with breast cancer. Part of the blurb reads: 'What begins as their need to know the facts about cancer becomes, as the years pass, a highly personal enquiry into what it means to be alive. To face the uncertain future and to accept death'. It's in this spirit that we should address Peter Max Kandhola's images of his father. How could he not look at someone he loved so much, even in death!

2002

NOTES

1 This text was written before the coronavirus pandemic.

2 Christian Boltanski discussing his work *Les tombeaux* (*The Tombs*, 1996), www.museoreinasofia.es/en/collection/artwork/tombeaux-tombs.

3 Julia Kristeva, 'Approaching Abjection', *Oxford Literary Review*, Volume 5, Issue 1-2, 1982, pp125-149.

4 Pedro Meyer, narration from the CD-ROM *I Photograph to Remember*, 1991.

Photography:
Promises to Make
a Revolution

31

In Five Short Acts

Paris, 6th January 1839. We have much pleasure in announcing an important discovery made by M. Daguerre, the celebrated painter of the Diorama. This discovery seems like a prodigy. It disconcerts all the theories of science in light and optics and, if borne out, promises to make a revolution in the arts of design.

M. Daguerre has discovered a method to fix the images, which are represented at the back of a camera obscura; so that these images are not the temporary reflection of the object, but their fixed and durable impress, which may be removed from the presence of those objects like a picture or an engraving.

The Literary Gazette, 7 January 1839.

Act 1

The industrialisation of human trafficking by European imperial powers has left a profound *visual imprint* on the modern world. The lack of recognition of indigenous cultures and epistemes, which have been negated and misrepresented in the West as uncivilised and savage, is a defining marker of the Western colonising era. The refusal to see the Other as subjects in their own right and on equal terms has been made manifest in centuries of literary and visual material, becoming part of a Eurocentric homogenous construction of world history that places the West above the rest. These dark histories, when peeled back, reveal the development of Western visual practices against the Other that violently and systematically codified 'racial' and cultural difference. An analysis of the making and circulation of the Other within Western image production through the application of photography, especially from the mid nineteenth century onwards, exposes the politically and visually problematic position the Other was placed in within the field of Western representation.

Throughout the eighteenth and towards the middle of the nineteenth century, Europe's Enlightenment artists were concerned with creating aesthetically pleasing works that represented their world as being balanced and in harmony with nature. Through neo-classical forms of representation, the European artist rendered 'his' world and 'his' history, as he imagined it. The violent realities of Western imperial power and genocidal practices were denied in Western art practices. As a result, nineteenth-century images relating colonial encounters become imagined moments of great European conquest. The art academies in Europe mainly concerned themselves with debates on the relative values of the portrait, history or religious painting over that of landscape painting, or on the place of the artist as genius in an academy of image production that effectively cloaked the violence of the colonial project in myth, fantasy, denial and disavowal.

Act 2

Reason or 'objective truth' in aesthetics, ethics, science and government was the ideological backbone and justification that underpinned the continuing development of the European imperial project. According to David Harvey, the underlying principle of the concept of the modern world was

> to use the accumulation of knowledge generated by many individuals working freely and creatively for the pursuit of human emancipation and the enrichment of daily life. The scientific domination of nature promised freedom from scarcity, want, and the arbitrariness of natural calamity.[1]

The advocates of Enlightenment theories and scientific methods became preoccupied with justifying their belief that Aryan culture was superior. They could not imagine a world of co-existence with the environment, different societies and cultures. Difference, especially concerning black Africans and indigenous tribal peoples of the South, was equated with inferiority. Inferiority conferred the obligation to be observed by the imagined superior European race, which then classified and indexed the Other using scientific modes of scrutiny that were based on Eurocentric and therefore universally defined empirical knowledge systems. Photographic images of the Other produced by Europeans across photographic history reflected this preoccupation with superiority, reflecting a sense of European entitlement.

Photography grew rapidly to become a popular form of European image-making. Three months after the invention of photography, daguerreotypists were operating out of Egypt. Photography had effectively entered Africa and was fast becoming the preferred mechanism employed to support the representation of European desires of, and perspectives on, Africa. The invention of the camera within the global climate of racial politics in 1839 and the European desire for colonial conquest was to have dire consequences for how the African subject would continue to be framed within Western regimes of representation.

Act 3

By the 1860s, the camera had become part of a vital toolkit for scientific encounters with the Other. Anthropologists and pseudoscientists alike quickly embraced the new opportunities offered by photography and systematically trained their cameras on their 'native' discoveries. The results of these encounters would rapidly be accumulated and form a global archive of photographs that would later be housed as formal knowledge systems in museums across Europe and North America. One can surmise that Africa's exposure through the lens of the European camera created an accelerated form of African cultural erasure in the eyes of European people. Photography made culture in Africa static and fixed in time.

The camera in the hands of progressive scientists/anthropologists and colonial officers literally laid flat all that came before them. Once the camera was focused on the 'uncivilised' subject, and with the centralised guidelines offered by the colonising photometric systems, photographs effectively began to play a critical part in the process of cultural obliteration. Cultures that existed outside recognised forms of capitalist expansion, that operated under different value systems and were not dependent on material gain, were denied a sense of cultural worth and made invisible. This is evident in the treatment of non-European peoples who, as we can see through the archives of Europe, were stripped bare before the camera.[2]

Anthropological photography allowed the Other to exist in another place, a place that, in effect, had little or no relevance to the actual indigenous cultural values or experiences of the people who were photographed. The Other was photographed but was never portrayed. The resulting images taken by the colonial camera formed an archive that reflected a desired, imagined superiority that would render invisible complex heterogeneous societies that operated outside of European understanding or need. The desire to consume the Other, to make the Other exist within the same system as the coloniser, is a fundamental function of colonial rule, where the ideological imperative is to negate difference and to convert people's lives, spaces and ways of being into slaves.

The intensity of the desire to classify and control the Other extended to sections of Europe's own societies designated as inferior or subhuman. Europe's colonial gaze turned inward on the weak, the vulnerable, the infirm, the mentally ill, the disabled, the poor, the criminal and the working classes, and any other human subject that could be designated Other. All were subject to Europe's increasingly violent gaze and genocidal sciences. Through the establishment of eugenicist theories and practices by scientists such as Frances Galton and Alfred Ploetz, people would be forced into the frame, measured and debased before the lens and other instruments of deadly medicine that signalled the path to the death camps of Europe.

The circulation of anthropological types of photographs showing indigenous tribal people in periodicals such as the *Journal of the Anthropological Institute*, and the cultural context immediately before and after what came to be known as the 'Scramble for Africa', aided and endorsed the case for colonisation of the continent. The Berlin Conference of November 1884-5 was a world defining moment and can be seen as the pinnacle of Europe's desire to obliterate the Other. For three months until 26 February 1885, Europe and the world's superpowers haggled over boundaries and rights within the interior of the continent, negating and making invisible the cultural and linguistic boundaries of the indigenous African populations. The use of photography by anthropologists and scientists in Africa mirrored the overall political objective that was mapped out at the conference in Berlin.

Terry Smith points out that 'practices of calibration, obliteration, and symbolisation'[3] were to become the dominant strategic forces in marshalling the visualisation of the black subject.

> Erasing the habitus, the imagery, the viewpoints, and eventually, the physical existence of indigenous peoples – these are the practices of obliteration. This may take the form of violent extinguishment or violation of ceremonial sites; of creating an environment in which the indigene can no longer live, leading to lassitude, a 'dying out' which puzzles its ignorant author; of unauthorised reproduction of Aboriginal designs to a literal scrawling of graffiti over sacred signs; of assimilating the indigene to the supposedly universal framework of Western

rationality or setting him and her at an unbridgeable distance
– as a 'Noble Savage,' for example. These practices range from
actual, brutal murder to an equally potent imaginary othering.[4]

There is no form of European colonisation that has not attempted
indigenous cultural erasure. Extensive anthropological photographic encounters reveal little about the character of the subject
in the frame. On the contrary, the images produced through the
colonial offices provide for us, in retrospect, detailed information
concerning the perspective of the colonial camera. In an inverted,
visual, anthropological sense, the photographs that were taken by
early European photographers now reveal more about the knowledge systems of those behind the camera than the subject in focus.
What is exciting about African photography now is that it is forcing
a reckoning with this hegemonic, colonial photographic gaze.

The photographs made by the colonial camera reveal that it
operated through a preconditioned set of cultural values that were
consciously or unconsciously mapped onto the Other. The ideological conditioning of the colonial photographer around the 1860s set
the visual frame for how the black subject was to be constructed.
Therefore the act of photographing the 'Other' in this context, no
matter what the objective scientific purpose, was to a vast degree
already predetermined by well-established visual codes and ways of
seeing and being. Through the socio-political framing of the African
subject in historical images that portray the relationship between
a black slave and white master, for example, the early nineteenth-
century colonial photographers (anthropologists, missionaries and
adventurers), believing in their God-given superiority, were destined
to produce an image that reiterated and mirrored their sense of place
in the world. Photographs produced and selected by early European
photographers therefore confirmed their imagined superior mindset
when addressing the Other. The Other was never photographed as
an equal.

Act 4

With the aid of photographs, the iconography of black inferiority within Western visual culture would, by the beginning of the twentieth century, come to be read as 'common sense'. Eurocentric dominance over photographic production and the circulation of photographs debasing the black subject have had enormous and deeply pervasive consequences throughout contemporary Western (and non-Western) societies. The observational photographic document became the authoritative representation of the black subject, continuing a tradition of black objectification that is rooted in Western art history. Images associated with imperial rule and scientific photography operated on an industrial scale, especially through the proliferation of world fairs in major European cities, such as the ones held in Paris and London after 1850.

Scientific racism saturated anthropological, scientific and medical journals, travel writing, and novels, these cultural forms were still relatively class-bound and inaccessible to most Victorians, who had neither the means nor the education to read such material. Imperial Kitsch as consumer spectacle, by contrast, could package, market, and distribute evolutionary racism on a hitherto unimagined scale.[5]

The implication of debasing images circulating at world fairs was that millions of people had access for the first time to racist images of black people. According to Timothy Mitchell, by '1889, to give an indication of the scale of this process 32 million people visited the Exposition Universelle, built that year to commemorate the centenary of the Revolution and to demonstrate French commercial and imperial power'.[6]

Act 5

Delinking the stereotype, challenging the photographic canon and contesting the dominant ideology of Western history has, in recent years, been a key site of contestation for decolonial activists, theorists, artists and photographers. It has mainly been through the direct anti-, post and decolonial struggles that developed in China, India, Southeast Asia, Africa, and the Americas, especially post-World War Two, Europe's ultimate colonial war, that we can begin to witness the control of image and text by Europe being challenged, both from within the West and simultaneously from voices speaking from political and cultural perspectives in the global South. It is clear that indigenous counter-narratives can have the capacity to challenge and agitate the established historical canon of photography; however, it should also be recognised that radical counter-narratives can be incorporated by proponents of the canon as a form of academic reanimation which, through its position of power, can absorb criticism and consume difference as a strategy for maintaining visibility and power.

The creation and recognition of counter-narratives across photography works as a discourse in its own right, disrupting the centre and challenging the conservative flaneurs of photography. They offer signposts to possible new forms of cultural understanding in our time, and new ways of thinking and delinking from the violence of the past, pushing us to consider further the work images do in culture. They help us see that which is not known or has been suppressed, but which is often felt.

This article first appeared in Beyond III - [post]colonial Present *in May 2020.*

NOTES

1 David Harvey, *The Condition of Postmodernity: An Enquiry into the Origins of Cultural Change*, Blackwell: Oxford, 1990, p12.
2 In 1995 I worked on a project with The Photographers' Gallery titled

The Impossible Science of Being: Dialogues between Anthropology and Photography which investigated this. See also Malek Alloula, *The Colonial Harem*, Myrna Godzich and Wlad Godzich (trans), University of Minnesota Press: Minnesota, 1986.

3 Terry Smith, 'Visual Regimes of Colonization: Aboriginal Seeing and European Vision in Australia', in Nicolas Mirzoeff (ed), *The Visual Culture Reader*, Routledge: London, 2002, p483.

4 *Ibid.*, pp483-4.

5 Anne McClintock, 'Soft-Soaping Empire. Commodity racism and imperial advertising', in Mirzoeff (ed) *op.cit.*, p508.

6 Timothy Mitchell, 'Orientalism and Exhibitionary Order', in Mirzoeff (ed), *op. cit.*, p495.

32

Lumumba Framed in Colonial Time

30 June 1960 marks the day that the Republic of the Congo gained its independence from Belgium. Tragically, the date also marks the beginning of the end of an idealistic form of nationalist politics that enabled Patrice Lumumba to become the first democratically elected Prime Minister of the newly formed sovereign state. Many European journalists were present to witness this defining moment of liberation for the Congolese people. Robert Lebeck, a young German photo-journalist, was among them. He was working on an assignment for the German magazine, *Kristall*. The photographs that Lebeck made in Leopoldville on 29 and 30 June 1960 have now become important photographic markers concerning the representation of this turbulent transitional moment in Congolese and Cold War politics.

Lebeck's Leopoldville independence photographs, when read in the present, perform incisive, critical and unsettling historical work. As images, when read through the prism of race, time and decolonial thought, they have the capacity to become charged indicators that point to the past codes of Belgium's violent colonial oppression. Reading Lebeck's photographs enables us to consider the deadly and destructive colonialities that were at work on the Congolese people. We now know that Belgium, while allowing the Congo to proclaim independence, was simultaneously pulling the new Congolese state towards the dark theatre of Cold War politics and internal conflict.

Lebeck's photographs work not only as historical records of Congo's day of independence, which is inherent in the time of their making; as photographs, they are, by design and desire, images made to translate the essential codes of Eurocentric photo-journalistic meaning. The 'who', 'what', 'where' and 'when' are all codes that suggest news is being made through the photograph. Now, as time does its work on Lebeck's photographs, these images evolve from news-related objects into indexical cultural signifiers that visually prise open the past for contemporary interpretation. As Congo's independence on 30 June 1960 becomes unstoppably distant and temporally locked in colonial time, Lebeck's photographs now aid those who wish to drill deeper through the hard bedrock of colonial history. As photographs, they pause the present and free the past. They contribute now to new understandings of colonial time because, like all photographs, Lebeck's are not closed fields of knowledge. What lies outside the frame, culturally and politically, bears heavily on what we see within any documentary moment. Photographs travel through time at varying velocities of discourse and affect the production of knowledge within the different temporalities, politics and locations of their reading. Photographs that do important historical work have infinite and slippery punctive markers. How we read photographs will depend on the knowledge formations that surround them.

The archives of Lebeck's Leopoldville photographic moments invite us into a process of much needed political and visual archaeological work. Who and how we sift through the archives of our time impacts critically on what knowledge is circulated, valued and kept alive. The archive, when read through decolonial time, is effectively opened up to different voices, and through those different voices becomes a contested space for knowledge formation. Rearticulating photographs from the past enables us to exhume the ideological and ontological nature of what has been buried or disappeared through acts of colonial violence. Examining the visual moments of colonial encounter archives such as Lebeck's helps us to act upon and understand the critical condition of European colonial disavowal. To perform forensic work on the consciousness of Europe's past, particularly concerning the colonial era, we must first encourage an act of European self-recognition regarding their relationship to visual forms of cultural violence in the making of Others. This process will undoubtedly generate different understandings of the complexities at work when we consider the psychology of European colonial denial within the epistemologies of visual culture and history-making. This form of cultural reconstruction work may well enable new knowledge concerning the colonising mind to surface. Its only when this new, self-reflective knowledge concerning the internal, un-seeable trauma of colonial violence is recognised by the colonisers that there can be an acknowledgement of the full extent of the violent ontology of Western thought.

As photographs being read in the present, Lebeck's images work as turbulent reminders of the past visual precursors to the violence that was to befall the Congo just a few months after its independence. Any signifiers inherent within Lebeck's photographs that represent autonomy, respect, political gain or freedom from the grip of colonisation are made tragic, melancholic and redundant when examined in retrospect. How, for example, can we examine in the present a photograph of Patrice Lumumba in his office of Prime Minister without bringing forth a conversation that addresses the extreme and violent nature of Lumumba's death? Knowing that Lumumba along with two of his political associates, Maurice Mpolo and Joseph Okito, within months of being elected, were taken to an isolated spot in Katanga, shot, buried and then shortly afterwards, under the orders of the Katangan authorities and their Belgian counterparts, 'dug up, cut into pieces ... then thrown into a barrel of sulphuric acid'.[1] This knowledge alone makes looking at photographs of Lumumba an act of resistance against the violent, colonial desire to disappear him and his politics entirely, literally dissolving any trace of Lumumba's physical being. The treatment of Lumumba therefore represents an example of extreme cultural erasure at work.

Photographs of Lumumba from Lebeck's archives, especially those of him in office, now haunt, in a most traumatic way, the political consciousness of the West. They become evidential, visual placeholders that highlight

> the true nature, not only of the former colonial powers, but also the United Nations, of the recently independent countries united in what was called the Afro-Asian bloc, as well as of Moscow and finally the national elite in the Congo which bowed its head to the Western offensive against the Congolese Government.[2]

The photographs that Lebeck made in Leopoldville offer the viewer an opportunity to consider the phenomena of racial time at work in history, how race marks the past and locates the future, particularly when we consider the struggle of those who wished to be nonaligned to either Russia or the United States. The different temporalities a photograph produces can chart the degrees of unrestricted colonial entitlement present at the time of an image being made. Therefore, Lebeck's photographs from 29 and 30 June 1960 become unique registers against which we can begin to examine the damaging and totalising effects of Belgium's colonial rule on the Congolese and indeed the Belgians themselves.

Photographs of Lumumba taken on the day of independence invite us to consider the dark political reality of what was unfolding in the Congo under the guise of independence. The ideological and political differences concerning the formation of the new Congolese state is where the fault line of understanding occurs between the old European colonial power and the new nationalist agenda of Lumumba. Belgium, like many other colonial powers, did not and could not imagine or manage the process needed to be able to transition out of its toxic state of colonial domination.

The power exercised by Belgium as a former colonial master was not in any real terms being transferred to the Congolese people. A neocolonial recalibration of the Congo was critical, as far as Belgium was concerned, so as to guarantee the continuation of the violent processes of extraction and oblivion that had historically been at work on the Congolese people, and which formed part of Belgium's sense of post-independence entitlement. Lumumba harboured deep dissatisfaction concerning the violence and abuse his people had suffered. This was clearly evident in the unofficial speech that Lumumba delivered at the Congo's independence day ceremony. He stood, uninvited, on this day and claimed his right to have a voice, reminding the new nation of the immense indignities his people had borne during Belgium's seventy-five years of colonial rule. Through his speech, broadcast by radio across the nation, he was determined not to negate the historical violence which the Congo had been subjected to. Much to the discomfort of King Baudouin I and the other Belgians present, Lumumba evoked the Congolese people's traumas when he reminded the people that morning, noon and night we were subjected to jeers, insults and blows because we were 'Negroes'. Who will ever forget that the black was addressed as 'tu', not because he was a friend, but because the polite 'vous' was reserved for the white man? … Who will ever forget the shootings which killed so many of our brothers, or the cells into which were mercilessly thrown those who no longer wished to submit to the regime of injustice, oppression and exploitation used by the colonialists as tool of their domination?[3]

For Lumumba, the first act of liberation was to fully recognise the dehumanising experience the people of the Congo had suffered. This recognition of human suffering would signify the end of colonial time and the start of a journey to humanity.

One photograph taken by Lebeck on the 30 June warrants special attention. It's a photograph that illustrates how time, race and politics function as competing dynamics. The photograph portrays Patrice Lumumba at the official luncheon that was held to mark Congo's independence. All the dignitaries from the independence ceremony were due to attend the event. We can see from the untouched cutlery and rolls of bread along with the clean, empty glasses that the photograph was taken before the luncheon had started. Lumumba is framed in the lower foreground of the photograph, his left hand rests relaxed on the table and his right hand appears to be searching for something below the line of the brilliant white tablecloth. Lumumba appears to be feeling for something inside his jacket pocket. However, it's his expression that creates the punctive moment of drama within the photograph. His gaze is hard and is directed towards his right and his mood appears to be sombre, dark and heavy – Lumumba is clearly troubled. Lebeck has framed Lumumba in a moment of immediate post-independence isolation, caught in thought or trapped in political conjuncture as by the time this photograph has been taken, Lumumba would likely have been made aware that King Baudouin I had felt personally humiliated by the content of his proclamation speech and wanted to leave the celebrations. The Belgians clearly preferred a historical narrative that denied the death and destruction at the core of the colonial presence in the Congo, desiring instead a version of history that presented the Belgians as a benevolent and kind, civilising master.

Lumumba himself was surprised by the strong reaction the Belgians had to his speech[4] and it was only through the intervention of the newly appointed Minister of Foreign Affairs of the Congo, Justin Marie Bomboko, that King Baudouin I agreed to stay at the ceremony. Bomboko had assured King Baudouin I that Lumumba would clarify the content of his earlier speech during the forthcoming luncheon. Here, through the prism of Lebeck's photograph, we are able to consider the weight of responsibility to both the past and the future that Lumumba was burdened with in this critical moment. His earlier speech had received extended applause from the Congolese in the audience. However, this same speech had isolated him from the Belgians and also the Congolese political elite, who felt a responsibility to their former colonial masters for the way the transition to independence was registered across the new sovereign state and within history. Ominously, within the background of Lebeck's portrait of Lumumba we see several blurred, out-of-focus figures gathered on the steps of The Palace of the Nation. We can make out the presence of several suited African men along with several other African men who are less formally dressed. Also faded and out of focus in this group are two military personnel, each functioning within the photograph as external props in which Lumumba's head is framed. These military military personnel, when read now, become ghostly presences that foretell the role the military were to play in Lumumba's death. Within the aesthetic of the photograph, the military men are a visually upsetting presence as they draw the viewer's eye away from Lumumba towards the dark-suited, unknowable figures standing behind his back.

This photograph has one last visual episode for us to consider. In its top right-hand corner, we can make out the presence of a European subject who is partially obscured by the architecture of the Palace. His presence disturbs the scene as he functions visually as a subtle reminder of the colonising past very much present in the backdrop to Lumumba's future.

2017

NOTES

1 Ludo de Witte, *The Assassination of Lumumba*, Verso: London and New York, 2002, p141.
2 *Ibid.*, p181.
3 Patrice Lumumba, Speech at the Ceremony of the Proclamation of the Congo's Independence, www.marxists.org/subject/arica/lumumba/1960/06/independence.htm, accessed 23 November 2021.
4 Thomas Kanza, *The Rise and Fall of Patrice Lumumba: Conflict in the Congo,* Penguin: London, 1972, p225.

33

The Photographs of Eustáquio Neves

In 1995 I was invited to Brazil to present a paper, 'On Photography and Identity', as part of the Second International Photo Meeting '95 in São Paulo. During my short visit, I was to conduct some informal portfolio reviews with photographers, mainly from the São Paulo area. I had been informed by colleges at NAFOTO, a photographic agency based in São Paulo, that a photographer was making his way to the meeting place especially to see me. He was travelling by bus overnight, making the long trip to São Paulo from Minas Gerais. The photographer's name was Eustáquio Neves and I had an impending sense of responsibility and nervous anticipation whilst awaiting the encounter – I was worried that Neves could be making a wasted journey. However, my anxieties were proven to be misplaced. Neves presented me with some of the most innovative photography I had seen and I remember the encounter with great affection.

By 1995, Neves had already completed two major bodies of work, *Urban Chaos* (1995) and *Arturos* (1993-95). In *Urban Chaos*, he begins to investigate a theme that he will return to again and again: social inequality. *Urban Chaos* is a series of constructed photographs that portray nihilistic, abstract cityscapes that evoke the nightmares of a post-apocalyptic world. The photographs present us with a veil of tension. The surface of the work is distressed with time marks and layered with dystopian meanings. Neves's construction of the city represents the harshest of all environments for humanity to exist in, a place where hope seems to have been abandoned, inverted and left for dead. The photographs from *Urban Chaos* signpost the deprived existence and hardships that millions of city-dwellers globally have to endure in order to survive. It is as if the series were launched from some past Dadaist moment to remind us that beneath the veneer of social progress and so called development lies an underbelly of mass disillusionment, shattered existences, polluted atmospheres and chemical rivers.

The series *Arturos* was made in 1993-94. In this series of photographs, Eustáquio Neves lays claim to his desire to make contact with and celebrate the African in Brazil. The works are complex visual narratives that lay history before us and at the same time celebrate the present. *Arturos* the series references the injustices of slavery and highlights the strength, discipline and value of the Arturos community's spiritual life. These photographs affirm and testify to the power of self-respect. They celebrate the deep-rooted sense of identity within the Arturos community.

There is an intense sense of pleasure and identification with being African in the *Arturos* photographs. Through this series, Neves opens the door to a world that is almost beyond race and into the domain of deep faith, where he invites us to enquire about the nature of the spiritualised world and the complexities of Christianity in relation to Africa and its diaspora.

Arturos is a reminder of the need for, and social function of, ceremony in society and how ceremony is catalytic in the binding together of communities. *Arturos* is, in of itself, a shrine to a people that exist as a sacred family, deeply connected not just through biology but also through experience. Through the *Arturos* series, we see a people who not only understand the nature of struggle but who, through faith and strength in collective identity, have also managed to survive. *Arturos* is quite simply a beautiful visual alchemy of religious and cultural meanings. The work is loaded with the contentions produced by history, religion and power that are rarely allowed to coexist.

Eustáquio Neves's later works based on football produced around 1998 comment once again on social conditions. Football, 'the beautiful game', is played under a haze of urban mist and oppressive city pressure. Every available patch of land that could be used to play on is being imposed on by the threat of crushing urban expansion. The footballers even have to compete for space with recently washed clothes. Trains run within touching distance of the sidelines and apartment blocks push upwards in competition for fresh air. The sense of claustrophobia is agitated by Neves's refusal to allow us to see clearly. In looking at this series of photographs, you cannot help but feel that the grime and grit of the city is being kicked up in your face. As the dust metaphorically settles, the eyes are left deliberately irritated by the overall bleakness of the scene. 'The beautiful game', once a signifier of global harmony, is rendered ugly. The players in the mist represent the vague possibility of something better. Neves's football series pays homage to those who dare to play and try to win against overwhelmingly negative social circumstances. The young men in these images have, in many instances, already lost. The circumstances of their birth have ensured that the result of their life's game is a guaranteed struggle.

In Eustáquio Neves's more recent work there is growing sense of unease. Issues relating to race, representation, colonialism and postcolonialism are now paramount to his photography. When he arrived in London in winter 1999, he spent many days wandering around Brixton. He said at the time, 'In Brixton, I identify with places, people and everyday activities. As I wander around with the critical eye of a researcher and the admiration of a foreigner, I feel a sense of belonging'.[1]

There is a sense that colonial history, for Neves, has not been reconciled, and he is deeply troubled by the current state of black people in contemporary Brazilian society. From the very beginning, the issue of inequality has been at the core of his practice. He is acutely aware of the relationship between black people and commodification. Neves's very existence in Brazil is testament to the exploitative nature of global trade. It is no wonder, then, that as Neves's work matures, themes of social injustice return again and again to haunt us through him.

Eustáquio Neves is the past manifest in the now. He comes from the place of re-memory, a place that can't be ignored. Neves has to, by the very fact of his blackness and his concern for socio-political change, take on those who can't see past the surface, the epidermal schema of things. 'The fact of blackness', Professor Stuart Hall reminds us, 'is that which will not go away'.[2] Neves is compelled by his very condition to remind us all of the circumstances he operates in: this is a racialised world.

Later works from 1999 onwards take a more directly confrontational approach, as Neves starts to map out key themes within

his photography. He begins to examine and deconstruct the objectification and exploitation of the black body: advertisements are
exposed for their blatant disregard for the black female body; old
documents and newspaper articles announcing the escape of slaves
are juxtaposed with job advertisements that are coded to exclude
black applicants.

The iconography of the slave trade begins to emerge in Neves's
photographs with a powerful presence and new confidence. Neves
takes the genocidal violence of colonialisms past and equates it to
the current political global situation. His work entitled *Other Slave
Ships* (1999) reminds us of the awesome capacity of globalisation
to impose awful conditions on the majority of the world's citizens,
while at the same time recalling that imperial power has been built,
to a large degree, on the violent exploitation of African peoples.
Neves therefore asks us to consider what has changed as he reminds
us that the contemporary condition of slavery takes many forms.

Neves has decided not to ignore the very specific conditions of his
position in Brazil. He's not locked in a new, post-conceptual debate.
His work is clearly directed at and engaged with the conditions of
blackness, and he acknowledges that those myriad conditions can't
be expressed without recognising the need for ancestral dialogues.
Artists such as Rotimi Fani-Kayode, Albert Chong, Carrie Mae
Weems and many others share Neves's concerns. Weems, Chong,
Fani-Kayode and Neves, all in their own specific and individual
ways, allow memory to be active in the construction of the now.
Neves's desire is to recycle the past into a manageable memory for
the future.

It is not surprising, then, that after spending time researching at
the Slavery Museum in Belo Vale County in the state of Minas Gerais,
Neves felt compelled to photograph the brutal metal punishment
masks. Sometime later, taking an image of his mother, he morphs
the mask in set stages onto his mother's dignified portrait until she
is completely obscured by it – effectively silenced and objectified.
It's in the series *Punishment Mask* (2004) that Neves finally reveals
to us how deeply and personally he feels racial oppression. The work
in many ways is his most violent and deliberate – he literally masks
his own mother.

This essay was first published in a catalogue which accompanied the exhibition Mostra Pan-Africana de Arte Contemporânea *at the Museu de Arte Moderna da Bahia, São Paulo, Brazil, in 2005, produced by Associação Cultural Videobrasil e Fundação Palmares.*

NOTES

1 From a conversation I had with Neves in 1998 while he was in residence at Gasworks and Autograph, London, UK. Brixton is one of the key areas of black settlement in London.

2 Stuart Hall, from an audio-visual, multi-screen presentation for Les *Rencontres d'Arles*, 1993, titled 'Rencontres Au Noir: Black British Photography in the 80s.' Produced by Autograph (Mark Sealy) and *Ten.8* (Derek Bishton).

34

What Have 'We' Done with
the Image of Africa?

The very notion of Africa is complex. Few other geo-political spaces have been so highly contested. The idea of Africa has driven Europeans mad with greed and crazy with the desire to deliver both 'benevolence' and 'civilisation'. Exploiting African resources – or saving Africa from Africans – has been a concern for Europe's enlightened classes throughout time. Denying the entangled cultural relationship between Europe and Africa dates back through classical studies. Martin Bernal's recent series of contentious books titled *Black Athena* worked to expose Europe's classical studies as being inherently racist. After receiving much criticism for his work, he later stated that 'the political purpose of *Black Athena*, is, of course, to lessen European cultural arrogance.'[1]

The theory that the seat of civilisation is located in Africa is a historical scab on the knees of Europe that keeps being knocked off and won't heal. If we then begin to think about African history, culture and politics as a series of progressive ideologies then we enter into a dangerous and contested ideological arena, one that questions the very foundation of European ideologies. It's therefore increasingly clear that the invention of Africa, or our understanding of Africa, is implicitly linked to, and cannot be separated from, the way we have been invited to see Africa. Since the invention of photography in 1839, the medium has played a crucial role in how Africa has been rendered for Western consumption.

The legacy of how Europe constructed the image of Africa and its diasporic peoples remains an ongoing academic exercise. The outstanding cultural work we therefore need to do in the field of academia and in praxis is to develop a deep critical analysis of the psychological state of those who framed Africa, its peoples and their cultures so negatively.

Europeans, in a perverse, self-obsessed sense, may have become deluded, ill or driven insane with what they imagined Africa to be. The result is that the historical encounter between these different cultures, rather than being seen as connected and part of the world's story, has left the European moral economy completely bankrupt. The overriding result of European encounters with Africa are division, arrogance, denial and an imposed cultural and racialised hierarchy that remains genocidal in nature.

I therefore reject the notion of an African photography. What could it possibly signal and what is its purpose beyond geography? I prefer to examine the conditions of image production within a wider sociopolitical context, delinking from the confines of Western photographic history, which is bent towards maintaining the European canon.

Delinking work aids an imaginative curatorial exercise for the future, one that is open to different forms of enquiry and delivery, one that addresses the visual aspects of Africa without the smog of Eurocentric judgment clouding its reception and benchmarking its progress. The European curatorial photographic exercise in Africa is burdened with its own oppressive history, sense of purpose and ideological fault lines that have, over time, looked away from the face of the Other and employed a tragic, scopic regime that has objectified and damned Africa to a meaningless set of contradictions, stereotypes and polarities. The image of Africa made in Europe is therefore a mirror-like theatre that reflects not what is learned or shared with African cultures but what is suppressed and expedient from the encounter.

When we discover that there are several cultures instead of just one and consequently at the time when we acknowledge the end of a sort of cultural monopoly, be it illusionary or real, we are threatened with destruction by our own discovery. Suddenly it becomes possible that there are just others, that we ourselves are an "other" among others. All meaning and every goal having disappeared, it becomes possible to wander through civilizations as if through vestiges and ruins. The whole of mankind becomes a kind of imaginary museum: where shall we go this week-end-visit the Angkor ruins or take a stroll in the Tivoli of Copenhagen?[2]

When we look at the photographic works of Zanele Muholi, Uche Okpa-Iroha and Saïdou Dicko, what we see are not resolutions, not great testimonies of truth. We are not being presented with liberal, humanitarian photographic clichés. These photographs work because they offer us a mosaic of the world in which we are all connected.

Muholi's series *Being* (2007) brings into focus the intimate and quiet moments of black lesbian women's lives in South Africa. The photographs work as an extended conversation on love, tolerance, acceptance and pleasure. They also challenge the notion that lesbian love is a colonial cultural deposit that is un-African in nature. These photographs, which I presented in Toronto in 2010 through the exhibition *Bamako in Toronto*, address the urgent need to visi-bilise that which is taboo or driven underground in South African society, namely the simple fact that black African women do love, care and build meaningful relationships with each other, and need to do so without the threat of violence from either fellow citizens or state agencies. These images do more than frame contested, local, forbidden desires; they demand attitudinal change on a global level.

Muholi's photographs, when viewed as political statements, protest that this community is present, resilient and no longer willing to marginalised. The photographs stand out as sensuous and tender, life-affirming moments, victorious in their subjects' sense of 'being' in the everyday. In describing the intentionality behind these photographs, Muholi states,

> As a visual artist, one is always confronted with the politics of representation. I have the choice to portray my community in a manner that will turn us once again into a commodity to be consumed by the outside world, or to create a body of meaning that is welcomed by us as a community of queer black women. I choose the latter path, because it is through capturing the visual pleasures and erotica of my community that our being comes into focus, into community and national consciousness. And it is through seeing ourselves as we find love, laughter, joy that

we can sustain our strength and regain our sanity as we move into a future that is sadly still filled with the threat of insecurities – HIV/AIDS, hate crimes, violence against women, poverty, unemployment.'[3]

As moments of activism, these images categorically remind viewers that enshrined within the constitution of the Republic of South Africa are legal guarantees that protect its citizens against homophobia. They call on the state to perform its duty to affirm and protect the rights of all its citizens, no matter who they choose to love.

Uche Okpa-Iroha's project titled *Under Bridge Life* (2008) is a series of atmospheric photographs that also work as campaigning agents. They offer an insight into the violent social conditions that the disenfranchised peoples of Lagos live with. Okpa-Iroha photographed under one of the main bridges that connects the affluent Lagos Island to the mainland. The photographs are presented as a sequence of dramatic, dream-like images from a murky, underworld place that is home to thousands of people living in unregulated conditions. Within the images, people appear as ghosts, drifting through a darkness occasionally interrupted by bright shards of sunlight that enter from gaps in the structure of the bridge.

The blurring of subjects works for Okpa-Iroha, as he deliberately wanted to avoid the pitfalls so prevalent within victim-orientated documentary photography projects. There is no need for closeness when the atmosphere is so violent. This work is a direct attempt to shift the dynamic in terms of representations of poverty. Here, those traditionally rendered nameless within photography of poverty are deliberately absented.

In making his subjects present but not identifiable, what the viewer is offered is a set of images that align with the politics of resilience and resistance of the world's poor. What's captured through the series is an atmosphere in which people survive despite the harsh conditions they are forced to endure. *Under Bridge Life* prevents the gaze from focusing on any specific individual. Seeing the broken black body in state of anguish is, for Okpa-Iroha, a redundant, tired trope manufactured under colonialism. Instead, Lagos is joined here with many of the world's other megacities. It becomes part of a global network of aggressive capitalism that increasingly cares less for its most needy citizens and provides for its elites through policies of exploitation and degradation of the poor. These photographers then represent an important, indigenous African voice, one that begins to divest from the tragic African image bank that is so pervasive throughout European culture. They collectively open another account for the way the image of Africa can be presented.

Saïdou Dicko's work *World Mosaic/Mosaïque monde*, produced between 2005-09, comes together as an archive of 600 colour photographs, each 4 x 3 inches, displayed in an interconnected, grid-like formation. The focus of these photographs is on everyday moments of people's lives, not through a direct portrayal of the human subject in focus but through the shadows they cast on the world as they move through the sunlight of their day.

In *World Mosaic*, Dicko has built an archive of small, endless stories that are only made present through the shadows cast by people and the objects they are connected to. Here, the narratives of each sequence have no beginning or end, they are moments in the time of the day caught by both the camera and through the sunlight, leaving the viewer to imagine the nature of the subject producing the shadow image. Rather than attempting to fix the subject in the present, what Dicko does through his emphasis on framing shadows is to highlight the transient nature of human presences as an interconnected, global and unifying daily affair.

In *Bamako Encounters* (2009), through the work of photographers such as Muholi, Okpa-Iroha and Dicko, and the many others present at the festival that year, there was an overriding sense that photography as a tool for social change was being owned by a younger, more militant generation of practitioners. The exhibition, staged at the Gladstone Hotel in Toronto in 2010, produced a curatorial sampling of the works of Zanele Muholi (South Africa), Uche Okpa-Iroha (Nigeria), and Saidou Dicko (Burkina Faso), all of whom, in their different approaches to image production, challenged the status quo of photography's past by reclaiming the who, how and what an image of Africa might be in their present and in the future.

This text accompanied the exhibition Bamako in Toronto, *held 3 June – 2 August 2010 at the Gladstone Hotel, Toronto, Canada.*

NOTES

1 Paul Vitello, 'Martin Bernal, "Black Athena" Scholar, Dies at 76', https://www.nytimes.com/2013/06/23/arts/martin-bernal-black-athena-scholar-dies-at-76.html, 23 June 2013.

2 Paul Ricoeur, *History and Truth*, Charles A. Kelbley (trans), Northwestern University Press: Evanston, 1965, p275.

3 See http://archive.stevenson.info/exhibitions/muholi/being.htm.

35

Les Bijoux I-IX (2002), Maud Sulter

The influential historical painter Paul Delaroche, on reviewing some daguerreotypes, made his much-quoted remark that, 'from today, painting is dead.'[1] Charles Baudelaire, the poet and critic, was equally agitated by the development of photography, and referred to it as merely a product of industry.[2]

Over 160 years later, photographer Maud Sulter has produced *Les Bijoux* (2002), a series of confrontational and sensuous self-portraits that acknowledge the important role that Jeanne Duval, Baudelaire's black mistress, played in his creative and personal life.

The key function of *Les Bijoux* is to remind the viewer of how critically close African and European cultures have been throughout history, and that the complexities of these encounters cannot be reduced to simplistic understandings of white encounters with the Other. In many respects, Baudelaire was dependent on Duval, but history written from a Eurocentric perspective denies the nature of this relationship. Duval is therefore reduced to the margins and literally erased.

Sulter's *Les Bijoux* is named after one of Baudelaire's most celebrated poems. These self-portraits function as a reassertion of the presence and power of Jeanne Duval, the black mistress who financially supported and inspired some of his most important works. This representation of Duval is an essential form of cultural excavation, bringing Duval back from oblivion and repositioning her. Sulter's *Les Bijoux* reframes Duval as an independent and forceful influence on one of France's greatest poets.

Gustave Courbet's celebrated painting, *The Painter's Studio: A real allegory determining seven years of my life as an artist* (1855), hangs in Musée d'Orsay in Paris. On close scrutiny, this painting reveals the faint trace of Duval's presence next to the seated figure of Baudelaire.

Duval's erasure from Courbet's work occurred apparently at the direct request of Baudelaire who, after falling out with Duval, demanded that Courbet remove her from this major new painting. Courbet, aware of Baudelaire's influence as an art critic, duly obliged.

The question of Duval's erasure is a major concern for Sulter, as it marks the intensity of the relationship between Africa and Europe and is symptomatic of the relationship between the two continents. *Les Bijoux*'s sense of redress allows the historically rendered, culturally absent black woman to have a voice. Through this form of photographic production, the viewer is allowed access to a new perspective that shifts the imbalance in relation to how black women have historically been portrayed and heard.

In the guise of Duval, Sulter deliberately emanates an alluring sense of confidence, and within each photograph in the series there is a strong undercurrent of sexual power. This is intensified by the possibility of both violence and rejection as Sulter, posing as Duval, turns away from the camera or tugs at the jewels on her neck, thus breaking with the conventions of desire. Collectively, the images undress the past and expose the condition of one who has been rendered invisible.

This text first appeared in Next Level, *No. 12, 2007.*

NOTES

1 From the catalogue for *The Beginnings of Photography* at the Victoria & Albert Museum (16 March – 14 May 1972), Arts Council of Great Britain: London, 1972.

2 Charles Baudelaire, *Mirror of Art: Critical Studies: Charles Baudelaire,* Jonathan Mayne (ed, trans), Phaidon Press Limited: London, 1955.

36

How Does the South Appear on the Art Empire's Map?

The Venice Biennale has for over a century been one of the most prestigious cultural institutions in the world. Established in 1895, the Biennale has an attendance today of over 300,000 visitors at the Art Exhibition.

The Venice Biennale website, www.labiennale.org

At 72, Malick Sidibé is the undisputed master of his photographic generation. No artist anywhere is more deserving of the 2007 Biennale of Venice's Golden Lion for Lifetime Achievement, and none more worthy of being the first African so honored.

The Venice Biennale press release, 15 May 2007

The Guggenheim Abu Dhabi is the largest museum in a series of cultural institutions planned as part of the Saadiyat Island Cultural District, which will serve the world as a destination for the advancement of knowledge and the understanding of culture through the arts.

The Guggenheim Foundation website, www.guggenheim.org

The legacy of colonisation and racism still worries the European present. It will not go away. It resurfaces as a morbid reminder of the intense level of cultural violence that was aimed at the Other over centuries. This cultural violence has left a profound visual imprint on all aspects of the modern world. The deliberate refusal to see those constructed as Other as being subjects in their own right defines a literary and visual legacy that has become part of the dominant

Eurocentric construction of world history. Although theorists and critics have exposed this reality, there has not been a reduction in its operational power: the lack of recognition of indigenous cultures, which have been historically misrepresented in the West as backward and savage, is a defining marker of the pre- and postcolonial eras. But aesthetic modernism – that amorphous obsession of Western art history – almost never registers either the violence of colonialism or the erased subjectivity of the so-called native. And whenever art from the South is discussed, it seems that anxious discussions about what modernism was, when it occurred and how it continues to resonate are never too far away.

Be that as it may, Europe and North America still continue with the tired cultural business of display and discovery. If we attempt to discuss cultural difference in this framework – or to develop a critical movement within photographic and visual art practice – we quickly reach the dead end of a systematic negation of art institutions altogether: in practice, a self-silencing. It's also important to note that the globalisation of the art world has resulted in a new category of of artist, the professional Other, who, causal as you like, will claim the position of being post-race, afro-politan, or alter-modern, depending, of course, on whatever curatorial opportunity presents itself. Chameleon-like practice has now taken centre stage. What is left of and on the margins?

The imperial North has historically taken charge of controlling the means of visual production and has constructed a worldview that is founded on Western mythologies: white supremacy, white originality and white historicity. These mythologies are designed to bolster the hegemonic power of the North, and now are focused on creating a Southern clone: replicas in 'exotic' locations that are designed to ultimately mirror cultural industries of Europe and the US. Eurocentric ideology is fundamentally dependent on the propagation of canonical figures that sustain control across global cultural sites. This allows for the interpretation of cultural exchanges to be seen primarily through Eurocentric modes of articulation. Negating difference by ultimately setting Western modernism as the norm, a grand Eurocentric construction of art history and cultural management is created and marketed in the form of a 'mirror' South. Is it enough to move from one stage-managed Southern location to another, or place the Southern puppets in mock conversation, when an excessive and seductive 'art empire', which ultimately holds court at Venice, continues to pull the strings?

Eurocentric visual culture helps to maintain colonial and neo-colonial hierarchies through the control of representation, projecting a form of imperial benevolence that sustains traditional power relationships. Those of us who are concerned with issues relating to the North-South cultural divide need to examine just how much of the art produced in the South is aimed at Southern audiences, and who composes these Southern audiences. What is the ratio of North–South image flow? What is presented and by whom? Under what conditions? How could South-South exchanges challenge these asymmetries when they continue to circulate between institutions modelled on the Northern art world, funded by Northern sources and often marketed to Northern tourist audiences – or Southern audiences performing modernity by aping Western aesthetic tastes?

I would argue that it is therefore logical, indeed necessary, to analyse artistic production not just in geographical or racial terms, but in terms that fundamentally seek to investigate how power works and who is ultimately speaking for whom. Unhinging the stereotype, challenging the canon and contesting the hegemonic perspectives of the West has for many years been a constant site of conflict for postcolonial activists, academics, artists and freedom fighters. It's only through direct anti- and postcolonial struggles that developed throughout Asia, Africa, and the Americas – especially during the highly charged Cold War years of the 1960s and 1970s – that we begin to witness the Eurocentric dominance over the image and text being contested. This opening has been achieved mainly by those with an understanding of what it means to be positioned as Other, those who speak from a subaltern perspective, a space of difference.

There is a danger in grounding a critique merely in the assertion of cultural difference from the West. Imperialism has systematically innovated, expanded and applied visual technologies, and created institutions through which images could be critically positioned and consumed – not only for the power of surveillance and control, not only to erect models of colonial subject formation, but in order to create the Other as historically and temporally distant from the European. In the emperor's court, this distance is maintained today by displaying artists from Africa, Asia and the Caribbean primarily within ill-defined, sweeping geographical contexts, rather than according to political frameworks, aesthetic tendencies, historical currents or other meaningful curatorial criteria. Art galleries, universities, and museums – and crucially, reproductive print media, archives and collections – safely incorporate art from the South by assimilating it to depoliticised categories (including, sometimes, 'the South') that deflect our vision from historic and contemporary forms of institutional and structural violence.

The adoption of a 'post-race' position goes much further than simply reducing art to a market position. It leaves much of the harsh, violent reality of Western imperial power invisible, once again erasing the dark side of cultural progress. The cynical cults of diversity, cosmopolitanism, and the professional artist-Other underwrite the 'Art Empire' by producing a contaminated knowledge, a sanitised and 'enlightened' inclusiveness, ultimately based – like an earlier Enlightenment universalism – on the conviction of superiority. We must ask: does the South exist as a location? Or is it, rather, a set of conditions, a product of systemic violence and ideological domination? Who can claim the right to represent this condition? To whom? And on what basis?

This essay was first published by Justina M. Barnicke Gallery in the catalogue South-South: Interruptions & Encounters, *Tejpal S. Ajji and Jon Soske (eds), which accompanied an exhibition by the same name from 2 April – 19 May 2009.*